More *than a* MILE

MICHELLE PARKER

LifeMark Ministries
2500 Dallas Parkway, Suite 495
Plano, TX 75093

ISBN: 978-1-944058-06-7

To my mom and dad
who gave me roots and wings
and the loves of my life
who share my nest.

Meet MICHELLE PARKER

A love of words, conversation and seeing God at work in the routine of daily living drives most of her days. As a stay-at-home mom, those passions converge on a daily basis. Whether participating in Bible study or watching her son play at the park, Michelle believes that every experience provides opportunities to grow closer to God.

Born into a military family, home was defined by the *people* not the *place*. The current place is Texas and the people are the absolute loves of her life — her husband Kevin, two grown daughters Claire and Mallory, a full-of-energy little boy named Joshua, and a furry pup named Riley. In addition, in both the current and past places – including Iowa, North Carolina, and Virginia – God has given her the great gift of enduring friendships.

When not tackling the duties of motherhood, Michelle can be found with a book in her hands, having coffee with a friend, or on the phone deep in conversation with friends all over the country.

To learn more about Michelle and her journey, visit the website: www.MoreThanAMile.org

The JOURNEY

As a little girl, you could find me climbing trees or riding bikes or playing kickball in the street with the neighborhood gang. I ran around outside all the time! In high school, I played a sport every season. I was never the star of the team but always a team player. An active lifestyle is just a way of being for me.

While I enjoy movement, I've always been casual about my chosen activity — nothing too hard or strenuous. And the one aspect of movement I've always disliked? You guessed it — running! I could go fast but never long. When I would hear people say they were planning to run a marathon, my first thought was "CRAZY!"

So how is it I came to run a marathon?

I realize that God often asks of us obedience not in areas that come easy, but in those areas where we have doubt. He points us in directions we know we cannot go without the help of a knowing God who can take us places that are beyond us.

The idea of the marathon really evolved, and at the beginning, I had no idea how it would progress. It began with running, actually putting one foot in front of the other and moving forward. It also began with prayer. A single verse chanted over and over as I took step after step. I had no real "plan" initially, but as I ran and my mind cleared, God taught me that it was less about running and more about the ***process***.

The plan for how I would get from mile 1 to mile 26 unfolded, and I allowed God to lead the way. In the circumstances of my life at that time, I began praying for people, then that prayer fell into a rhythm as I passed each milestone — mile 1, mile 2, mile 3... the pattern of prayer matched my steps and made running bearable. It wasn't until the 5th mile that the idea to ask someone for a verse really took hold. After that, it began to make sense that each mile would stand alone and represent someone I was praying for. As I ran that mile, I would pray for that person and their particular needs, one mile at a time. Of course, Cheryl was mile 1, and she was prayed for every time I put on my sneakers.

When we let go of our need to control and allow God to place before us the plans as He sees them, amazing moments take place. He meets us in our need and supplies us with His strength to get the job done. This is not done without work or struggle or even doubt. What I found, though, was shared work and shared struggle and less doubt as I progressed in my journey.

For my friend Cheryl, her marathon was cancer. She went to doctor appointments and chemo treatments and surgery rooms. She did not choose her marathon and had she been given the choice, I think she would have said, "no." For me, I chose running. God called me to obedience in a plan I did not understand and I said, "yes" — reluctantly. But in that yes, God poured into me lesson after lesson of how running and faith can mirror each other...how "hard" places can mold us and teach us in ways that "comfortable" places never can.

We all have a purpose — each different and unique in the plan God has for our lives. For six months one year, I said yes to God's purpose, that He might lead me and teach me for all the next seasons that would come. My hope is that in the lessons I learned, you too can apply them to your "marathon." Maybe your marathon is running like mine but more likely, your marathon looks like infertility, divorce, child struggles, a job loss or a million other human struggles that we face. No matter what your marathon is, it is a place that cannot be solved today. It is a journey that will likely last for weeks, months, or possibly even years!

This book has been written as a 30-day journey, and each "day" has 3 sections. The first section is who the mile was dedicated to on my marathon, including a little about them, how we know one another, and the verse they selected for me. These were the people who traveled the miles with me. The second section covers the lesson I learned in that mile. Some were in training and some on the actual marathon day. The last section is for you, for your marathon. It includes a few questions to help you think and consider and then a page to journal, pray and hear God's voice.

You may be wondering how a 26.2 mile marathon is a 30-day journey – good question! I've added two days before and after the miles to give you some additional background information and help you reflect on your own personal marathon. In addition, the lessons learned in my journey were written "real time" when I experienced them. Even though they are now in the past, I have chosen to leave them as they were written so that you will feel like you are in the middle of the journey with me!

In the actual running of the marathon, I was SLOW — it took me much longer than it took others — but I didn't care about the time. I say this for you as well. If 30 days is too fast, then slow down and go at your own pace. My prayer for you is that you would allow God to take control, lead and direct. Your part is to listen, obey, and trust. The journey is great, but our God is greater!

Let the journey begin...

Your JOURNEY

Our journey through life will likely include multiple "marathons" — challenging circumstances that push us beyond what we can handle on our own. Take a moment to consider your current "marathon" and where you are in your journey. Write in the journal space the answers to some of these questions:

Where are you in your journey?

What "marathon" are you facing and how do you feel about it?

Are you overwhelmed? Scared? Unsure?

"Within each struggle, there is a blessing waiting to happen."

- Joyce Rupp

5

Before WE BEGIN...

For most of my life, I've been in a battle with my own body — not with the way it functions, but with the image I see reflected in the mirror. God's Word tells me that my body is a temple and God made me exactly how I am. I know these things and try to honor them, but this is where the struggle gets difficult...in the gap between what God says and what my own eyes see.

This is also where the need for exercise was born. I've always played sports, and when I became an adult, I belonged to a gym and took classes. My exercise routine has always been sweating and socializing. The social part is how I made it fun...but it left me feeling like it wasn't enough...like I was missing something. This was when God gave me the idea of **purposeful** exercise.

This was the seed for a journey that was greater than the distance of 26 miles. Through the course of this journey, I discovered how to endure long, hard roads and how to lean into the goodness of God — He meets us right where we are. He uses different "marathons" in life to teach us and grow us — not for punishment or control, but to bring us into perfection. Perfection not in the worldly sense, but in His eyes. Some years ago I wrote down this quote by Kathleen Norris,

"To 'be perfect' in the sense that Jesus means it, is to make room for growth, for the changes that bring us to maturity and ripeness. To mature is to lose adolescent self-consciousness so as to be able to make a gift of oneself as a parent, as teacher, friend, spouse. Perfection, in a Christian sense, means becoming mature enough to give ourselves to others. This sort of perfection demands that we become fully ourselves as God would have us: mature, ripe, full, ready for what befalls us, for whatever is to come."

I want this kind of perfection, as God would have it. However, before I could strive for this, I had to clean house. I had to find the places in my heart that needed work and ask God to help with the heavy lifting. It hurts when we understand things about ourselves that are not-so-pleasant, but in order to grow and mature, that identification has to be done.

The "cleaning house" that took place during my journey uncovered other areas of weakness, and I can better appreciate how God has been patient all these years. You see, areas where I'm challenged in other ways are structure, discipline, a love of sweets and finishing long projects. I can see clearly now that all these years of watching what I put into my body and movement on a weekly basis had made me strong. It made it possible for the health of my inside to accomplish things I've set out to do.

So it made sense to me that when Cheryl's body was failing her, God would ask me to challenge mine. To use what He had given me (a healthy body), to honor Him and to suffer a bit. Oh, He is gentle in the process of teaching us!

As I trained for the marathon, I had to use all the areas of weakness that I had struggled with my entire life. I had a training plan for everyday and I knew that if I didn't prepare daily, then race day would be even harder — that required **structure**. On days that I felt pain or discomfort, I had to figure out how to press forward — that required **discipline**. On days where I wanted to skip veggies and indulge in delicious treats, I remembered that sugar was not my friend — that required **healthy choices**. And when I was weary from all that needed to be crossed off before I would be done, I looked only at that day and kept moving — that required **completion**. Finally, when I was overcome with fear and doubt of what I had committed to do, I remembered that it really was not about me but what God could do through me — that required **faith**.

I believe God wants the best for us...that He wants us to love the person we are, in the ways He made us. We are gifted uniquely and purposefully and in the image of Christ. But we have to be open to the process...to the marathon He places before us. In the end, I understand that the things we struggle with the most bring the most joy when we've overcome them. What we realize is the process has brought us to new understanding and appreciation for what we regarded initially as pain.

Our job is simply to begin — to place a foot on the path and take one step and then another. God will meet you there. He will take your hand and catch you if you fall. So let's begin...together.

Your MILE

We all struggle with aspects that we don't like about ourselves. But we must remember that God loves us and that He created us — He knows us inside-out! Take a few minutes today and reflect on these questions:

What weak areas of your life need strengthening?

Read Psalm 139 and write down some of the things you learn about how God sees you.

Do you see yourself the way God sees you?

"We delight in the beauty of the butterfly, but rarely admit the changes it has gone through to achieve that beauty."

- Maya Angelou

9

MILE 1

Cheryl's MILE

My friend Cheryl is amazing. We met in college, were roommates for a short time, grew apart a little in our 20's, but found each other again. We've never lived in the same state since college, but we love to talk on the phone and see each other as often as possible. She has tons of energy, takes on challenges that amaze me and hardly ever complains. She has 3 kids, a military husband, a full-time job and 2 part-time jobs, and she would still cook you dinner or watch your kids if you needed help. She also has Multiple Sclerosis (MS) but hardly ever mentions it. Like I said, she's amazing!

When she called and left a message, it didn't occur to me that anything was wrong. No high-pitched voice or strange sound alerted me to anything other than just a call to catch up. But, she called back. She left another message: a routine exam had found a lump. My friend had cancer. I remember what she said when I called her back because it's so Cheryl... *"I don't have time for this right now — I have too much going on!"* She wasn't exaggerating. They were a month out from moving across the country, and they were facing a period of about 6 months of temporary living arrangements with their 3 small kids. And now, cancer...surgery, chemo, and radiation. In fact, the movers arrived only ONE WEEK after the surgery!

When I called to check-in after the double mastectomy, we had a conversation about what was going to be the hardest thing. That's when she said it...planted the seed. She said the real cancer marathon would begin with the chemo. It would be a six-month marathon, but she was up for the challenge.

You see, Cheryl is my "runner friend." On girls' weekends, she's the one who gets up early to go for a run while the rest of us are still in pajamas, sipping coffee. She's the one who works a 12-hour graveyard shift in the ER and then goes to the gym because she has an hour before morning carpool. She's the one who would think about cancer like a marathon to be finished!

If we lived in the same state, I would drive her kids or cook her dinner on days that she's not feeling well. I would bring her little gifts or tell jokes while the chemo dripped in. I would hold her hand. But because we live far away, I can't do for her those things I want to do. I began to consider how I would travel this with her from so far away. The idea...I would run a marathon for Cheryl. I would not just run it though, **I would run it in prayer with her, for her.**

> *I can do all things through Christ who gives me strength.*
>
> **Philippians 4:13 (NIV)**

My MILE

This is how it works with God and me. A thought comes into my head — it's usually somewhat radical and way out of my comfort zone! It's an idea that is just a seed with the phrase, "no way" attached at the end.

But it's the thing that keeps making it's way to the front of my brain and just won't go away. Then I say it out loud to someone and they don't look at me like I thought they would — like I'm way off-base. Next, I pray about it and ask God to give me yes or no answers. This is where it gets tricky.

Sometimes in that process, I get a clear no. Other times, I feel like I'm headed toward a yes, only to be surprised and disappointed with a gigantic NO. One such time was with the birth of my third child, Joshua (more on that story in Mile 4). The struggle of working through His answers can be messy and discouraging, causing me to doubt myself and question these ideas…but God keeps planting these seeds and through the struggle, my faith grows deeper.

I will begin with two important statements: First, I HATE to run! Second, God has a good sense of humor! After my son was born and I turned 43 (yes, in the same year) I finished an Olympic distance triathlon. I enjoyed swimming and really liked biking, but the running was the challenge. I really dreaded the run! So that's the first thing that makes this idea of mine crazy.

The second thing is that I've let myself go. We moved, I had a toddler, and my daughter had a year of surgeries — something had to give. What gave was my exercising, and my numbers on the scale automatically went up. Except for the latter months of pregnancy, I'm the heaviest I've ever been.

Despite these factors, I said this crazy idea out loud to my husband: "I'm going to run a marathon." Suddenly what had only been an idea became very real…and that's how this journey of miles began.

I begin each training run with Cheryl on my mind. When something hurts, I think of her — she can't quit chemo because it hurts! When I don't feel like running, I think of her — she doesn't get a day off "just because."

I never thought I would run a marathon. It's not something that was on my bucket list. Honestly, I never thought I *could*. Even today, I still don't really "want" to do it, but that is where God steps in and takes over. You see, Cheryl and I are close friends. We share history, motherhood dos and don'ts, tips on relationships, etc. But the most important thing we share — at the core of where we meet — is that we are sisters in Christ.

So I will run for Cheryl, with Christ, because… together, we are STRONG!

Your MILE

Don't allow frustrations with your own weaknesses to block you from progressing through the journey He has planned for you! God is so much bigger than you can imagine, and He will help you overcome.

Can you think of a time when God helped you accomplish something despite your own flaws?

If you are in the middle of your own challenging "journey," what markers have you made to identify your progress and help you keep moving forward?

"The secret of getting ahead is getting started"

- Mark Twain

Paula and I moved to Iowa within months of each other, and our daughters were in the same grade. This commonality allowed us to be at similar events, and over the past 10 years, our paths have crossed in various church groups, drawing us closer and closer. Ours was not a "fast friendship," but one that God chose to simmer and meld all the best ingredients together over time.

We both know something about the plans of God. We've both taken long journeys of faith where we knew God was in control but we could not see around the bend and had to trust Him. We had to trust that the future He had for us was filled with hope. He did not disappoint.

As I began the training for this marathon, Paula's husband had just passed away. When I ran, I began to pray first for Cheryl, and then for Paula. I thought about the plans of God and how even when they seem bad or unfair, God is at work. He is bringing beauty and hope into our lives, despite the difficult circumstances.

When I told Cheryl that I had selected Jeremiah 29:11 as my second mile verse, she said it was one of her life verses — one she had above her kitchen sink for years. It is a verse of dependence and trust for every journey we take in life.

"For I know the plans I have for you," declares the Lord, "plans to prosper you and not to harm you, plans to give you hope and a future."

Jeremiah 29:11 (NIV)

Race day is a culmination of choices and decisions made weeks, months, sometimes years before.

Beginnings are both exciting and scary. The wide-open possibilities and expectations of things unknown are exciting! But beginnings often require us to change something. They take what we've known or how we've chosen to operate and tip it over to create something else. Beginnings have nothing to do with comfort zones or calm places. But at the beginning of something new, we can't know the beauty of what is in store for us until we have movement.

I'm finding that as I tell people about this "race," they tend to ask if I have a goal time I'm trying to reach. So I began responding with, "I am a snail. I move forward slow and steady. I want to finish. I want to finish with a smile. That is my goal." When I told my husband that I might be the last person to finish, he cringed. But the truth is, crossing the finish line IS the goal.

God later brought this full circle when I was running my final long training run prior to the race. I woke up early after a night of slow, steady rain, and I headed out for a 13-mile run. As I neared the end of the first mile, I thought about how many times over these last few months I had been on this sidewalk. I remembered that this used to be hard and now it was my warm-up. I saw the places God had taken me and the people He had placed in my path. I thought about my goal of just finishing and not worrying about how long it would take.

As I looked down, I noticed dark dots covering the sidewalk. I had on brand new shoes and didn't want to get them dirty, so I slowed down.

As I stopped to see what covered the sidewalk, I started to laugh! You guessed it — SNAILS! They covered the entire stretch of the sidewalk as they just inched along! Of course, I stopped to snap a picture because God has the best sense of humor. He also has the most unique and creative way of saying, "Thank you for your obedience!"

Your MILE

Sometimes starting something new requires us to choose to have faith over our fears. The key to that is knowing WHO you have faith in — can you trust them to never let you down? God is faithful and will walk beside you through this journey if you'll invite Him — He will help you overcome your fears, and as an added bonus, He's great company!

Are you beginning a new season of life or facing a new challenge?

What fears do you have relative to your "marathon?"

What's one step you can take TODAY to help you begin?

"One does not discover new lands without consenting to lose sight of the shore."

- Andre Jide

MILE 3

God's MILE

That may sound a bit strange to call this "God's mile," but remember, I didn't set out with a grand plan when I started this journey...it just sort-of evolved along the way and became so much more than I could imagine! This mile wasn't about my friends or family. This mile was about God.

When the idea to run began in my head but before I committed to doing the marathon, I put my sneakers on and tried to run — the first day I could barely run a mile! Thanks to my year of inactivity, what had once been a simple activity was now very difficult and even physically painful. I decided I would take it slow and easy, so the 3-mile mark took a few weeks.

I have always loved Psalm 46:10 — it reminds me to just BE. It reminds me to honor God. It reminds me to breathe deeply. This seems appropriate for the 3rd mile because it is where the doubts begin to creep in. I'm far enough along for the reality of my idea to sink in, but I'm still so far out from the finish line that it seems impossible.

This is when I consider that I am truly crazy for thinking I can run a marathon, but that is also the place I remove myself from this equation, breathe deeply and allow God to step in. It's where I remind myself why I am doing this...for Cheryl. I chose a full marathon because by myself and for myself, I could not do it. But for Cheryl and with God, I feel like it is possible. Yes, I know I'm not physically "still" when I am running, but crazy enough, my mind is still and God speaks loud and clear. This is truly the only thing I actually enjoy about running — my time with God.

Be still and know that I am God.

Psalm 46:10 (NIV)

I love music. It speaks to my soul and fills my heart. In training for the marathon, it was the only way I could get through a long run — headphones on, music in my head. Three miles is a place I hit over and over in the months of training. It was routine, expected every time I put my shoes on.

I have a favorite musical group, Mercy Me. I know practically every song, and my iPod is filled with their music. Each time I buy a new CD, I read the summary of how they came to put the songs together. One of their early songs is called, "Coming Up to Breathe," and I had read that it was about being underwater then surfacing and taking a long deep breath.

That's exactly how I have felt after emerging from long, hard seasons. As if I had been holding my breath, waiting for God to move, waiting for Him to do something big. Months of running and praying had opened my eyes to miracles and answers just waiting to be found in ordinary days.

On my regular path, there's this beautiful tree in the middle of an open field. It may not look beautiful to some people, but to me it was "Cheryl's tree" — a visual reminder of the passing of time and the change of seasons. I saw it with leaves and I saw it bare. It always was a reminder that I was nearly done that day and to keep breathing. It also reminded me that God brings beautiful life back to barren parts of our journey over time. We must trust and keep moving forward with a stillness in our hearts that is in tune with God.

On this mile on race day, the music streamed from my iPod on shuffle because I love random. The "Coming Up to Breathe" song played, then repeated. My feet didn't stop but it did give me pause. In the rhythm of running, in planning, in the discipline, in working through aches and pains, in the support, in the asking for prayers...all these things allowed me to come up to breathe.

Breathe into my life the Spirit of God within. Allow Him to be seen in my action and in my obedience. It was in the action of doing what He asked me to do that I could BE STILL enough to see Him work.

Your MILE

In a fast-moving society, being still isn't easy or natural...but it IS invaluable! When we are still, we are able to understand others better, feel closer to God, and grow in His wisdom and life perspective.

When was the last time you were really still? Not just physically, but mentally and emotionally?

What did you learn about yourself in that time of stillness? What did you learn about God?

"Never be afraid to trust an unknown future to a known God."

- Corrie Ten Boom

This is Joshua's mile. He is 4 years old this year. This is the mile where I'm committed. This is where I remember that hard prayers require time and that the things we want most in life often evolve slowly. We are asked to practice patience and trust. The answer to Josh took 10 years.

For 10 years I prayed for a third baby, and in all that time, God kept sending me the Bible verse Joshua 1:9. One year, it was the central verse of our children's summer Bible camp; another year, it was part of a Bible study I was doing. In the years when I heard Him say no to my request, I would find this verse in my devotion or other books I picked up.

In 2010, Joshua 1:9 was the very first verse of the New Year in my devotional, and I read it having surrendered to God's plan in my life to not have a third child. I had asked and begged and pleaded with Him, and I'd heard Him say NO every time. Finally, I decided at age 42 that it was time to move on and begin asking for something else. I thanked God for a wonderful husband and two beautiful girls in my life and decided that was what God wanted for me. I realized later that month that **what God wanted was my trust in His plan and the surrender of my way and my timeline.** It was in my surrendering that God blessed me with a son.

Our Joshua is a fun, healthy little boy who is full of life. He is a beautiful gift from God, and he reminds me daily that God has so much more in store for us if we just wait for Him and follow His lead. Joshua truly was a lesson in God's perfect timing.

I was to run 4 miles out and back today. The catch was that the last 2 were supposed to be faster then the first 2. First of all, I run slowly (remember the snail?!). My fast pace is probably most people's slow pace. By 3.5 miles, I was sucking wind and doubts began to creep in. *"Are you crazy? Do you really think 26 miles is a reality when 4 is this hard?"* This is also where I have to summon all the positive I can find. **This is where God and I met today.**

My third verse is "Be still and know that I AM GOD" so between gasps of air, I chanted this and focused on the music. The song that began playing "randomly" on my iPod was by Laura Story, *Make Something Beautiful*. I found myself singing the lyrics and letting go, trusting Him to make something beautiful when I can't see His plan. If you aren't familiar with the song, I encourage you to check it out!

The words poured over me, and before I knew it, my GPS gal said, "4 miles." I looked up and I was on my street — I had made it! As the Mile 4 verse came to mind, I was reminded that I had to give up the dream of having a third child before God made that dream a reality. I must release my will to God's will, trusting Him to make something beautiful with my life. This trust process doesn't happen overnight — it happens one step at a time. I am not going to be able to run 26 miles overnight. I just have to do it one mile at a time.

Along my journey, periodically God whispers encouragement that I'm exactly where He wants me to be — strong and courageous to press on because my God is with me! As I sat on the step after completing this 4-mile run, I was consumed with thoughts of thankfulness. I looked up and a beautiful butterfly soared right over to me, paused, and then flew away. I am constantly awed that a magnificent God would meet me on a 4-mile run and whisper encouragement…I know He is making something beautiful.

> *Have I not commanded you? Be strong and courageous. Do not be afraid; do not be discouraged, for the Lord your God will be with you wherever you go.*
>
> **Joshua 1:9 (NIV)**

Life isn't about giving up on our dreams...it's about releasing them in order to allow us to gain a tighter grasp of the plans God has for us — a God who "is able to do immeasurably more than all we ask or imagine" (Ephesians 3:20, NIV).

What dreams do you need to release to God?

Do you trust Him to bring about something beautiful in your life, even in the midst of difficult circumstances?

"New beginnings are often disguised as painful endings."

- Lao Tzu

Nancy's MILE

This is the mile where the idea of asking others for the verses was formed. Nancy and I have been friends for over 20 years. We were pregnant with our first children together, 3 weeks apart. I was 2 weeks late and she was a week early, so my daughter and her son were born one day apart. We learned how to be moms together and navigated many of the "firsts" of parenting. We have not lived in the same state for over 16 years, but over the phone, we have covered many topics from toddler woes to college choices and everything in between.

She has always been the one to try new challenges in every sport from triathlon to mountain biking to skiing. I, in turn, have challenged her in spiritual ways by sharing my faith. For me, 5 miles was a big deal. As she was facing some changes in her life, I could see that we both needed to push each other in our strengths. I told her I was giving her a challenge to find the verse I would use to run 5 miles. I heard her sigh, but of course she came through. She chose 1 Timothy 1:7, and I think it speaks to who I see in her.

Oftentimes, just lacing up my sneakers is the hardest part of the run. I don't feel like running or it isn't convenient or the conditions are not ideal for running...I can come up with a million excuses. That is when I go back to a conversation that I had years ago with Cheryl.

We had been on a girls' trip, and we had just enough time for breakfast before we headed to the airport to return to our own homes and families. She appeared in shorts and sneakers and said she was going for a quick run. Soon after, she returned a bit sweaty and slightly flushed. I asked her why it was so important to run when she barely had time to eat and shower. She replied, "because I can."

This is how she marked what was important to her. It stopped me in my tracks.

In her twenties, Cheryl was diagnosed with Multiple Sclerosis. Despite the warning doctors gave her to reduce stress and probably not get pregnant, she has done what many healthy people never do. Not only did she have children, but she also continued to push herself and do the things she loved like running and competing in triathlons.

She didn't let her diagnosis dictate how she was going to live. Actually, just the opposite, her diagnosis gave meaning to the choices she made. She had faith that God would allow her dreams of healthy living and a family to emerge, despite the obstacles.

Cheryl is aware that one day this MS that is part of who she is may take over and affect her body beyond her control. So she decided to live with the mentality that "today I can and so I will!"

As I've trained and made choices that will affect how I will run, I think of this conversation often. Because of chemo and how it ravages the body, Cheryl can't run at this time...so I do. "Today I can" has taken on a much broader meaning. On days when I'm grouchy about lacing up my sneakers this is my mantra: "Today I can, today I can."

> *For God did not give us a spirit of timidity, but a spirit of power, of love and of self-discipline.*
>
> *1 Timothy 1:7 (NIV)*

Your MILE

Having the self-discipline to do what we know is BEST isn't always EASY — whether that's exercising, eating healthy, going to church, serving others, etc. Sometimes we delay what we "can" do just because we really don't want to. But once we push through the "I don't want to" feeling and develop good habits, it grows easier each time we choose to say YES!

With regard to your personal marathon, what things do you need to do today, this week, and this month just because you CAN?

What other changes can you make in your life that will improve the quality of your life, even though you may not feel like doing them?

"It is one of the most beautiful compensations of life, that no man can sincerely try to help another without helping himself."

- Ralph Waldo Emerson

Michelle's MILE

During my last year in Iowa, my friend Michelle and I trained for and ran a 10K in Colorado. We heard from friends that it was a great race, and we really just wanted an excuse to vacation with our families in Colorado, so we signed up. We are both laid back, easy-going people, so a date and a race kept us training. We ran in the cold (our coldest day was 0 degrees!) and in the rain and in the wind. We ran and talked and mostly, we just had fun.

On race day, we decided that we would run side-by-side. When she stopped or slowed down, so would I, and vice-versa. We enjoyed the race together. Our husbands thought we were crazy, but we knew that it was about doing this together, pushing one another to keep going and finishing with a smile. I had never run more than 6 miles, nor did I think I ever would. That is why I chose Michelle to pick my 6th mile verse.

Because I moved, I don't get to run with Michelle anymore. However, every time I hit the 6-mile mark I think of her and our great team effort. To me, life is about friendship. It's about helping someone out and traveling the distance with them. So that's it...mile 6. After this, I'm in brand new territory.

Take courage, it is I; do not be afraid.

Matthew 14:27 (NIV)

Last year, our daughter Mallory endured five major mouth surgeries. Time after time, I held my sobbing child as my heart broke right alongside hers. But I watched as God's hand was in every detail — both small and large. He revealed answers to each problem throughout Mallory's difficult journey — not in advance, but right when they were needed. In a sense, you could say that our understanding of the bigger picture evolved over time as God revealed more and more of His plans.

In similar fashion, He also revealed pieces of this marathon journey and Cheryl's cancer journey over time. Rather than overwhelm us with all the problems and answers at once, He allowed our faith to grow step-by-step. I never doubted, but each time the answer came, I still was amazed at how God could give comfort in such thoughtful and practical ways.

Sunday runs were beginning to make me nervous. They were beginning to get long and lonely, and I missed my Iowa running friend, Michelle. Then literally, I ran into a new friend, Laura!

I was walking with Josh early one evening, and Laura was running toward us. She recognized me from a newcomer meeting we had both attended, and we chatted for a few minutes. I asked if she was a runner, and her response was priceless. "I run, but not very fast!" Bingo! My new running partner was found! We made a date to meet on Sunday.

Our first run was 6 miles, and we talked the entire time! It was fun. Well, maybe not the running part, but definitely the friend and talking part! God knows our needs, in both the big and little details. Thinking about 20 miles on top of the 6 we just did terrifies me.

At the same time, I know Cheryl is scared thinking about all that is to come for every treatment. But together, we will knock it out one week at a time... sometimes one day at a time. I will face the miles while Cheryl faces the chemo treatments. We will do it differently, but we will do it in sync. God will meet us where we are and give us the people to help us.

Sunrise on the first morning I ran with Laura

The future may be scary and unknown to YOU, but GOD knows exactly what's ahead, so keep putting one foot in front of the other and trust the Lord to be with you each step!

Are you in "new territory?"

When you look to the future, does the unknown scare you?

"The truth is that our finest moments are most likely to occur when we are feeling deeply uncomfortable, unhappy, or unfulfilled. For it is only in such moments, propelled by our discomfort, that we are likely to step out of our ruts and start searching for different ways or truer answers."

- M. Scott Peck

33

The job I always wanted was to be a mom. While that has been my primary job for the past 21 years, I've always had some kind of part-time job. My favorite was working at my church when I lived in Iowa. It wasn't so much the job I did — it was the people I worked with. I loved these people — they felt more like family than co-workers.

Mary had a smile for me the first time I ever met her. She was welcoming and filled with joy. You could feel it just by walking into her office. She had a big job, but she never seemed too busy to help or chat or share a story.

In July, I attended her funeral where I discovered that I was not the only person who shared that encounter with Mary. The service was filled with hundreds of people who felt exactly the same way. She left this world the same way she had occupied it... *filled with joy.*

When she was going through chemo, one of her friends organized a group of friends to leave little gifts for her so that she had something fun to return home to after treatment. I had given her a CD by Laura Story called "Blessings." She had told me how much she loved it so every time I hear one of those songs, I think of Mary. As I was on a run one day, I heard the song, *Perfect Peace*. She came into my mind and I knew she was my #7.

I learned a few years ago that the number 7 represents completeness. Mary's journey here on earth has been completed, but the people she touched will continue to whisper of her life and all the beauty and joy she gave to others. Her husband Tom chose this verse so that I could honor her.

> *Let us persevere in running the race that lies before us while keeping our eyes fixed on Jesus.*
>
> *Hebrews 12:1b-2a (NABRE)*

My MILE

When I was a little girl, I thought of God like a year-round Santa Clause. I would ask for something "in prayer" expecting that I would get it. Age and experience have taught me otherwise, and my idea of God has changed for the better. I can see that in those childish requests, what I really wanted was peace...peace that I was ok...peace that I did not have to control every situation...peace to just be and not do...peace in the not knowing and not understanding.

I still ask in prayer for many things. However, now I realize that while sometimes God's answer is *"no"*, it is often followed by, *"but I have something else for you."* It is then that I trust. In some of those situations, I have seen with my own eyes the good things that God had in store for me in His own timing, like with Joshua when I waited 10 years for the answer to my prayer.

Still other times, like with Mary, we don't like the end of the story because it doesn't fit our earthly view. This is the divide between what we want and what God sees. It is where we struggle to find peace.

On the marathon, I hit mile 7 as I ran on the beach. The sun had just risen and it danced on the waves as they crashed onto the shore. The beauty of it slowed my progression and I searched the sand for shells to carry the rest of the way. I chose to not worry about time because it was more important to "be in the moment." It was as if a blanket of peace covered me. I got lots of stares from runners who thought I was crazy, but in

that moment, I felt gratitude that my body was able to move and breath and that my mind could pray and JUST BE.

Sometimes stopping for a moment to be aware is the only way we can connect the dots of where we have been and where we are going. When I can let go of the expectations I have for myself and the expectations others have for me, I find not an understanding of WHY, but an understanding of WHO. It's not about the yes or the no answer — it's about Who is beside me, Who knows the best plan, and Who I can trust. It is then that I feel what God promised, "Peace that surpasses all understanding" (Philippians 4:7).

"Why" questions can be consuming — they can drain us of our energy, our positivity, and our passion for life. But rather than allowing our focus to be on the WHY of our circumstances, we must choose to focus on the WHO...and it is a choice. We must determine in our heart and mind to focus on God's presence rather than our problems. It's a matter of the will.

Do you set aside time to disengage from the chaos of life?

Are you struggling with finding peace because of particularly difficult circumstances in your life right now?

How can you apply Philippians 4:6-7 in your life so that you experience God's peace?

"I long to accomplish great and noble tasks;
but it is my chief duty to accomplish small
tasks as if they were great and noble."

- Helen Keller

Tiffany's MILE

If I had any doubts about God being in the details of this journey, they were gone in this mile. Last year, my family chose to move to Texas. We were excited and ready, and we are happy that we did it. Having said that, moving is hard. . . change is hard! My realtor (who is now also my friend) said I HAD to come to her Bible study because I would love the ladies. She was right! In a world that was new and a landscape that was unfamiliar, it was the one part of my week that felt comfortable, week in and week out.

Little by little, I got to know the ladies in the group, and their families and stories grew familiar. I think what makes this group so wonderful is that we request and receive prayers from one another. This fall, Melanie (one of the ladies in my group) lost her daughter Tiffany in a car accident. I had not met her daughter, but I felt such sadness for Melanie and could only imagine her pain. As I ran a tough 4-mile run one Thursday, I heard clearly that Tiffany was my number 8.

I was unsure how Melanie would respond to my request. I'd been praying for her since finding out about her daughter's accident and subsequent death from her injuries. I think I was hesitant to ask her for the verse because I was so nervous to see her pain. But I had no doubt that Tiffany was my number 8, so I called Melanie.

I explained about the marathon, about the mile and Bible verses and how each person had come to me through prayer. I thought she might think I was crazy but I knew that Tiffany was to be my number 8. I also shared that 8 was a number in the Bible that represented new beginnings and that Tiffany's new beginning was Heavenly, despite the pain it caused here on earth.

We talked and cried a few more minutes and she said she had just brought some of Tiffany's things home, one of which was her Bible. She brought it outside to see if Tiffany had underlined a particular verse, and as we opened the cover we saw that she was given the Bible on Oct 8, 2008. The day we were having this conversation was Oct 8, 2014. We looked at each other knowing it was not coincidence that God led me to talk to Melanie on that very day. God knew that she had just recently brought Tiffany's Bible home and that she desperately needed to know that Tiffany was good...that she was at home — *her Heavenly home.*

"It's not all about you!" As a mom of teenagers, I've said this too many times to count. God often allows my mothering words to boomerang back to me! He asks us to be His voice, His actions, His comfort in real and tangible ways. Every time I prayed for Melanie and Tiffany, I understood that God was requesting this of me.

Coincidence really does not exist. What appears coincidental is really just an opportunity to hear God's voice.

These whispers from God become alive to attentive ears. They are moments of grace if we stop and recognize that God can step into our lives, into our breaking heart, into this world and give comfort.

God speaks if we will just listen. He does not leave us alone. He gives us occasions to reflect Him to others through our service and our love and compassion.

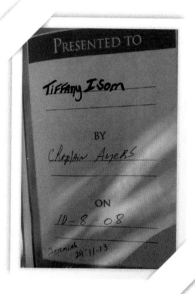

I feel so privileged when He asks me to act as His messenger, and I pray that I will continue to know His voice in my life and have the confidence to ACT on His guiding.

A word of caution: Although there are numerical patterns in the Bible, it's important that we see those patterns as a secondary story, not as the primary story. The FOCUS of the Bible isn't on the numbers...it's on the story of God's relationship with mankind through Jesus and the Holy Spirit. There's nothing wrong with seeing the significance of God in the details (like seeing the "#8" connection here), but I encourage you not to place the numbers or their meaning above the actual words and their meaning, as found in the Bible.

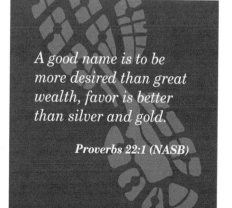

A good name is to be more desired than great wealth, favor is better than silver and gold.

Proverbs 22:1 (NASB)

Your MILE

When God prompts us to show His love and mercy to others, we must trust Him and step out in faith, regardless of how foolish we may feel. Remember what's at stake — there are more important things than our pride!

Is God prompting you to reach out to someone?

How can you act on that prompting THIS WEEK?

"For the most part, wisdom comes in chips
rather than blocks. You have to be willing
to gather them constantly and from sources
you never imagined probable."

- Anne Pachett

Mallory's MILE

This is my daughter Mallory's verse. I thought she was going to be mile 17 (because she is 17 this year), but no, she is my 9 girl. Did you know that there are 9 attributes that describe the fruit of the Spirit? They are: love, joy, peace, patience, kindness, goodness, faithfulness, gentleness, and self-control.

This past year has been rough for Mallory. Our move to Texas meant a new school, new friends, new house, new everything. In addition to moving, she has been through 5 major mouth surgeries and countless other procedures to fix something that was just a product of her genes. She had to face these challenges all while trying to navigate a teenage landscape that is hard enough on it's own!

When I think of the qualities listed as the fruit of the Spirit, I am amazed at how she reflects these qualities in her daily life, despite the difficult circumstances. She is a great example and encouragement to me to not only press on, but to do so with a heart that exhibits these qualities. At 9 miles, things are starting to hurt, but I've still got a long way to go. Cheryl is far into this cancer thing but still has a ways to go, too. I will practice and pray for love, joy, peace, patience, kindness, goodness, faithfulness, gentleness, and self-control.

Do not be conformed to this world, but be transformed by the renewal of your mind, that by testing you may discern what is the will of God, what is good and acceptable and perfect.

Romans 12:2 (ESV)

My MILE

I'm not a morning girl. I like the *idea* of early rising, but really I'm a "go-to-bed-late-and-sleep-in" person. In running, I learned that early morning is best and so what I've discovered is to find gems in the things I don't love. One Sunday morning was a great example of this...

I woke up for a short run and realized it was raining; it was still dark and with my clothes on, I got ready to get back into bed thinking I would just run later. My husband said, "You should run in the rain." So I did.

When I left the house, it was completely dark outside. I usually wait until it's light, but I'm trying to be considerate of my husband's morning workout, too. I've been running this stretch for over a month so I know exactly where the mile mark is. I was only doing 2 miles — short and fast. As I made the turn to return home, it was light. In that small window of time, the rain had slowed, dawn had come, and the view was magnificent.

It wasn't really a "sunrise" at all, though — it was like a gradual revealing of the day. Because it was still drizzling, clouds hung in the sky and the sun just peeked out behind them. My view was filled with colors of red and orange, places of both dark and light. As I looked to the west, I could see that it was still midnight blue as the sun had not made it there quite yet. It was a sky filled with contrast.

The struggles we are battling often feel like those places of darkness and light. They are seasons of life that are hard and require some patience. We cannot see beyond the clouds obscuring our sight, and yet, if we look to the sun — the real SON — Jesus, to give light to our darkness, we can begin to find the edges and outlines of what the eventual light will show. No true defining place that signifies the end and the beginning...just a gradual revealing...and the view is magnificent!

Your MILE

God will bring beautiful things out of our dark seasons of life if we're willing. . . but we have to allow Jesus, the light of the world, to illuminate the darkness.

Do you feel like your sky is dark right now?

Are you seeking God's light?

"Commitment unlocks the doors of imagination, allows vision and gives us the right stuff to turn our dream into reality."

- James Womack

MILE 10

Colleen's MILE

olleen once gave me one of the greatest compliments in my life — she said I was her "#10." Let me explain what that means.

My friend and running coach, Loran, has spoken often (I think he heard it in a sermon one time) about the 10 people who impact your faith journey. The first one is the person who first introduces you to the idea, and then throughout your life, others will come along and show Jesus to you until you finally see Him in action in your own life. Loran has always said that just once in his life he wants to be someone's "#10."

A group of girls were having this discussion one night at dinner for a friend's birthday and Colleen looked at me and said, "Michelle, you are my '#10.'"

Colleen was a friend that God had chosen for me, but I didn't know that when we first met. Our friendship began with common histories — we both moved a lot and were new to the area. We shared common schedules as our kids were in the same grade. Eventually, we knew our friendship was deeper through our common participation in church. We shared faith and struggles and how those two things weave together.

To me, a "#10" person is the one who ties the bow on the beautifully wrapped gift. It is Christ alive in us. It is the person who demonstrates and lives out faith in everyday actions and helps us to see "extraordinary" packaged as "ordinary." It is the face of Christ made evident. The fact that God would allow me the privilege to be that for someone (and then have the opportunity to know) is overwhelming and humbling. It gives me goose bumps!

Ten miles is a biggie, but if sharing my faith and love with Cheryl and with others is what I get to do with this marathon journey, then I will just keep going!

Therefore encourage one another and build each other up.

1 Thessalonians 5:11 (NIV)

In our family, we call it the curve ball. Everyone gets one! It's the thing you didn't see coming that changes everything — altering either your life or your perspective or sometimes both.

When I run, I have multiple routes depending on the distance I'm doing that day. I run with a GPS watch, water, sometimes food and my phone for music. I generally run in the morning, but occasionally I have an evening run because of scheduling. On one particular day, I decided to go off my route and head into a nearby neighborhood. I wasn't paying attention and got a bit turned around. Then my watch died. I still had my phone and I used my map app to get me onto a main street...and then it died, too! I realized I was some distance from home and had already run about 2 more miles than I was supposed to. It was getting dark, so I picked up the pace.

As I finally approached my house, both my watch and phone were dead, I'd been gone longer than expected, I'd gone through all my water, it was completely dark and I was exhausted from the extra mileage. I had to laugh at myself. I'd done everything I was supposed to do. I had taken my watch to keep me on track, a phone in case I needed help, music to keep me company and plenty of water for the run I had planned.

But here's the thing — sometimes things don't go as planned. Sometimes we can do everything right, and it still ends up wrong. Sometimes in life we get a curve ball — cancer, death of someone we love, an unplanned pregnancy or unable to get pregnant when that's all we want, divorce, kid issues — you name it, the list is long.

I remember when Cheryl called to say she had cancer and she said, *"I don't have time for this, it's not how my year is supposed to go."* That is so her! But sometimes we just don't have a choice — our only choice is how we accept the change of direction. What I learned that night as I finally arrived home is this: it's not about what the curve ball is, it's about how you respond. What is your perspective going to be? Will you gripe and complain that things aren't fair or will you just pick up the pace and find a path that is familiar and will bring you to safety?

On days that I'm not happy with my curve ball, I think of Cheryl. She sent me the picture below as she waited for chemo...see the smile?. It reminds me that in running and in life, **it really is all about perspective.**

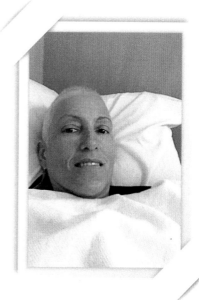

Curve balls throw off our equilibrium. They can cause anxiety, heartache, and many sleepless nights! But how we respond to curve balls has a longer impact on us and our situation. Seeing the difficulties that others are experiencing helps us adjust our perspective because we understand that we're not the only ones struggling.

Have you experienced a "curve ball" in your life or has someone you love had one thrown their way?

How will you respond?

How does it change your perspective when you come alongside someone else who is struggling?

"We can only be said to be alive in those moments when our hearts are conscious of our treasures."

- *Thornton Wilder*

y Mom and Dad gave me this verse. My favorite number is 11. It's my birthday (an important date to them), it was always my sports jersey number, and it's always been what I consider my "lucky" number.

I tell my parents (although probably not often enough!) that I hit the parent jackpot! I have been blessed to have parents who think I am wonderful. They love me as I am and have always allowed me room to become my own person. They've supported me in all things. They love my husband, my kids and my friends. They are my #1 fans. They planted the seeds of my faith, but more importantly, they showed me theirs to help me find my own.

Because they are part of my life, they know and love Cheryl, too. When I asked Mom if she would give me this verse she said she was honored and would be honored to pray for Cheryl. As I grow up, I want to be to my kids what my parents have been to me.

My MILE

I said this out loud on a Friday... *"Yay! I only have a six-mile run on Sunday."* That is a combination of words that I never thought I'd say!

I often look around me when I run, and observe God's creation — today was no exception. High in one of the bare, leafless trees was a small nest. When my daughter Claire was just three years old, she pointed out a nest to me...

We were driving along one dreary January day and I was thinking how ugly everything looked. I was anticipating spring and how beautiful the trees would be when they were green and full again. As this thought passed through my mind, my daughter sat in the backseat looking at the same scenery. However, she had a very different impression of that view. She said to me, "Mommy, you know what I like about the leaves falling off the trees?" I asked her "what" and she replied in that sweet three-year-old voice, "You can see all the nests in the trees when the leaves are off." I had never thought of that. I had never even noticed the nests in the trees. I looked at the empty branches and saw just that — nothing. But she saw beyond the obvious bareness to other possibilities. She saw fullness, hope, and life in the seemingly empty places.

From that day on, to me nests always represent hope and a new beginning. Cheryl will arrive on a Friday in December and two days later, we will run a half-marathon together to celebrate the end of chemo for her and the halfway point of training for me.

Her body will function for her, just not at the level it has been in the past. A hat will cover her short, cropped hair, but it is her beautiful smile that has not changed.

Despite the obvious bareness of this season (the outward appearances), it is her faith and God's provision that are the hope that shines from her and spills out to all those who know her story.

> *Train up a child in the way he should go, even when he is old he will not depart from it.*
>
> *Proverbs 22:6 (ESV)*

Are you in a barren season of life? Do you find your heart longing for spring? Instead of seeking the beauty that everyone can appreciate, seek the beauty that lies beneath the surface...go deeper!

What beauty can you see because of the barrenness of your circumstances?

How does focusing on the beauty revealed by barren circumstances change your perspective of these circumstances?

"Our chief want is someone who
will inspire us to be what we know
we could be."

- Ralph Waldo Emerson

MILE
12

Jenn's MILE

Jenn is the Assistant Director at Josh's preschool. She was the person who showed me around when my life was in complete change and chaos as a result of our move to Texas. Her phone call to say that Josh had a spot in the class was the beginning of a sense of order returning to my daily routine.

Each morning, she smiled as the kids came in and she knew them all by name. Her personal touch was a small comfort in a world that felt completely uncomfortable. Every afternoon as we left, she gave Josh a BIG hug goodbye. When someone loves your child, you just hold a special place in your heart for them. That's how I feel about Jenn.

As I neared the big miles, I prayed that God would place each person in my life and make it clear who I should be running for. Josh's teacher shared with me the news that Jenn had been given the dreaded diagnosis of breast cancer. Like Cheryl, a routine screening had started the ball rolling. I had noticed her absence lately, but this was not the news I was expecting. As I held her in my prayers, I approached my 12th mile.

In hearing and dealing with the news of cancer, Jenn and her family had chosen a Bible verse to commit to in this time of navigating unknown challenges while trusting in God's plan.

I was hesitant to ask her to be my 12th mile, unsure of how she would respond, but before I could even ask, I found out that she had chosen Romans 12:12 to be her "go-to" verse for her fight against cancer. That's right — chapter 12, verse 12! When I heard that, I got goosebumps because I knew that Jenn was indeed my 12th mile.

Be joyful in hope, patient in affliction, faithful in prayer.

Romans 12:12 (NIV)

My MILE

I saw this message on a sidewalk that was a little over a mile into a long run on a cool November morning: "He is Lord — He will meet you right where you are."

To say out loud "12 miles" seems laughable, but my sneakers are still hitting the pavement and I am moving forward. Just 6 months ago, it truly was laughable and even unimaginable. But I've come to understand and trust that **SMALL THINGS MATTER!**

In training, those small things are getting good sleep, taking in water, being prepared, and writing it down. Those are factors that make long runs possible. This is true in running as well as in life, including in your relationship with God and others.

Saying please and thank you to my husband and kids can change bossy and unappreciated around in a moment. Looking at the cashier or waitress and letting my gratitude for their job be evident shows kindness based on the person and not their status. Keeping some kind of connection to God is vital for relationship, whether it's quiet time or music or books or just the company I keep. These are the building block basics that make the long haul doable.

When the small agenda items get pushed aside and I allow just the "important days" to take over, it is then that I find the body breaks down... it is then that life begins to break down. On this journey, God met me right where I was. He said RUN and I will teach you the rest.

Sometimes He asks that I just sit still with Him — only then can I hear clearly the little things He has to say.

Your MILE

What an incredible truth that God will meet us right where we are — whether that's on a long lonely run, in a waiting room at the hospital, or on a couch in the middle of a quiet house. Wherever we are, He is right there wanting to encourage us. If we're willing to look, we'll see the little ways He reminds us of His presence.

Can you think of a time when God used something small in your life to encourage you?

What small changes can you make this week in your marriage? . . . with your children? . . . and most importantly, in your relationship with God?

"The best things are nearest...light in your eyes, flowers at your feet, duties at your hand, the path of God just before you."

- Robert Louis Stevenson

MILE 13

Iowa Friends' MILE

Moving from North Carolina to Iowa was a leap of faith for us — we literally didn't know anyone! Over the course of the ten years that we lived there, we made it our home and found people to share our journey.

It began with a group of guys working out together then having a morning Bible study...but it turned into so much more. This group became our family away from family. We vacationed together, shared meals together, and even celebrated holidays together. We helped each other in need and prayed big prayers of asking.

As I've mentioned previously, throughout this marathon journey, I have done a little research on the various meanings of numbers in the Bible. If there was significance to the meaning with relation to the stories and lessons in the miles, I journaled about that correlation.

When I looked up the meaning of the #13, one article described it as a number of blessing and change and a promise given and fulfilled. That's a perfect description of our time in Iowa. In the years we lived there, we tried to honor God in all the ways we lived. He placed in our life people who made us better and allowed us to grow in faith in real, everyday ways. Through laughter and fun and also serious issues, God revealed Himself in these friendships and fulfilled His promise with life's greatest blessing...the people with whom we share our days.

Iron sharpens iron and one man sharpens another.

Proverbs 27:17 (ESV)

My MILE

Before I began the race, I had a few "please no" requests of God such as "please no stomach issues" and "please no female issues." It wasn't a long list, and I thought it seemed reasonable. To avoid these while I trained, I made sure that every run was good practice for race day. I calculated calories and ate the same food before and during every run. So I felt confident that tummy issues would be avoided — the other one I really couldn't do anything about!

On the race, by the time I reached 13 miles, I had already visited several port-a-potties, and it seemed my first "please no" request would not be answered how I had hoped. However, my husband Kevin had met me on mile 9, and with him by my side, we laughed about my turbulent tummy and kept moving forward. I came to realize that even though I wasn't going to be able to *avoid* the things I feared the most, God was going to give me the help I needed along the way to *face* those fears.

I remembered that when I was pregnant with Joshua, I also had a few "please no" requests — mainly related to my desire for good health for my baby. Sometimes we experience the relief of having our "please no" requests answered just the way we hope. And sometimes we get exactly what we ask NOT to get!

Joshua was born seemingly completely healthy, but over time, we have come to find out that this wonderful bonus baby has a sensory processing disorder. There's

no quick fix or medicine to treat it — just a continual commitment to plow forward, pray hard, and trust in God's plan. And in all of this discovery, we have been shown the people who will help us persevere by providing knowledge, understanding, kindness, and laughter.

Once more, life and running mirror each other. Those "please no" requests have been turned on their side, and in getting what I thought I didn't want (the difficult path), I was given something more special and meaningful than I could have ever imagined! Don't be afraid to face your fears — God will give you His strength to get you through them!

Your MILE

We dread the difficult path, don't we? No one WANTS to get sick or WANTS to experience the pain of loss...and yet, when we accept our circumstances and travel the difficult path, our perspective often changes. We just need to be willing to step forward and face those challenges, trusting God to navigate the way through them. He will bring good from them sometime, though we may never fully see the ripple effect of the good He brings about.

Do you have any "please no" requests you've made to God?

Are you prepared to face your fears knowing that God will give you the strength and support you need?

"All men should strive to learn before they die, what they are running from, and to, and why."

- *James Thurber*

MILE 14

MOMS Group MILE

When Mallory was just 3 years old, I was part of a MOMS group. It was really the beginning of my personal faith awakening. Funny that 14 years later, I would be doing it again. I am different now — a bit wiser and more confident in my faith. But in other ways, I am exactly the same. The experience of being a mom, whether at 25 or 45, doesn't change.

I sat in class for 8 weeks and listened and learned and also shared my own truths. I asked them to pick a mile. They chose 14 because it was the date of our last class. It wasn't until later that I realized the personal significance — 14 was the number of years between mom's groups.

I was feeling a bit old and somewhat jaded. The book we used was exactly the same and in comparing my "younger self" with my most recent answers, I found that I haven't changed in the essential things!

Being with this group of women reminded me that the job of mothering is hard work and that in order to be successful and fulfilled, we need to find each other and stick together and reveal the truths God is teaching us.

It's a beautiful November morning after a week of icky weather, and I have an hour run. I settle in, listen to music and tell myself to just go. As I look down at the ground, I see acorns scattered around.

This year, I decorated the house for fall. Early in October, I purchased fall decorations and tried to make the house festive while Joshua was at pre-school. In Iowa, the outside did this FOR us — the trees would change and it "felt" like fall as the weather turned. But here in Texas, it's not as evident so I had to "make" it happen a bit.

I guess this is one reason I noticed the acorns on the ground. Just a week earlier, I had purchased fake ones to put in a bowl. They are big and round and "perfect" — I'd always seen acorns but these were oversized... or so I thought. I didn't realize acorns really grew that big so when I passed the real thing lying on the ground, I was surprised.

Because I was running an out-and-back, I knew I would pass them again and I had a while to think about it. Almost an hour later, I passed by and stopped to pick one up. It looked similar to those in the bowl, but you could see the obvious flaws. It was discolored in places and had a "hairy" cone on top and a few chips.

The one I held was alive and authentic. It is how I want to be as a person and as a Christian...the real thing. Christians walk around espousing that they believe and follow, but I want people to SEE that I am a Christian. When they meet me, I want them to SEE the light of Christ in me without really ever having to say it.

I plopped that real acorn in the bowl with the fakes. From a distance, no one would notice, but up-close, it's obvious. I will leave it and let it serve as my reminder to be authentic and real.

Strength and dignity are her clothing, and she smiles at the future. She opens her mouth in wisdom and the teaching of kindness is on her tongue.

Proverbs 31:25-26 (NASB)

Your MILE

Do you ever find yourself putting on a fake mask because you're afraid that if people saw the "real" you — flaws and all — then they wouldn't like you?

The Bible says that we are "wonderfully made" — that God handcrafted each of us in HIS IMAGE! How does that knowledge affect the way you see yourself?

If you have a Bible, I encourage you to open it to Psalm 139 and read what it says about you — then trust and believe it!

"Whether we are poets or parents or teachers or
artists or gardeners, we must start where we are
and use what we have. In the process of creation
and relationship, what seems mundane and
trivial will show itself to be holy, precious, part
of a pattern."

- Luci Shaw

Training for a marathon, I'm often asked if I run every day — No, thank goodness! I crosstrain and have a rest day as well. Keeping my legs moving without the constant pounding against the concrete is key, so I often ride my bike indoors. On one such occasion, the TV wasn't working where my spin bike was so I turned on the DVD player.

I popped in an old video of the girls when they were little. It was Mallory's second birthday party. As I rode, I watched images of old friends and their kids as they celebrated with us. Those babies are now in various stages of high school, college, and first jobs. I remember that day vividly and can hardly believe all those babies are grown up.

My 15th mile is one of those friends, Karen. We have been friends and mothers together for over 20 years. When we were young moms, our friendship was shallow and easy. Over the years, we've discussed temper tantrums and bedtime, navigated school choices and after-school activities, and talked about college options and career paths.

As the years of friendship added up, so did the depth of subject matter and support. As I look ahead, I see a friendship that will still be strong long after the kids have gone.

A few years ago, a mutual friend of ours passed away. I flew in immediately — barely having time to think through the loss. When Karen picked me up at the airport, I could not find words for my heartbreak. Arms wrapped around me as I cried, no words were needed. That is how I would characterize our friendship.

To me, that is what mile 15 is about… it's a long distance in, but still a ways to go. Even when we haven't talked in awhile, Karen and I can pick up right where we left off. Our friendship began with kids, but our shared faith is what has kept us close all these years. Words not spoken, but known. I hear her in this mile saying that she believes in me and I can do it.

I knew the 15th mile-mark would be hard. On this mile on race day, I was in a neighborhood running on tree-lined streets with very few spectators. There were a few other runners, but even those had dwindled since the only people left were doing the full marathon.

Years before I even knew it, God was planting friends in my life — people who would see both my best and my worst...people I would travel with...people who would speak truth into my life. It has been in the ordinary seasons of life (just as on this quiet street) that God has given me some of my greatest gifts — people who have shared my journey as God has taken me where I have never been before.

Sundays are long run days. I chose Sunday based on practicality because my husband is home, and I can get up early with little disruption to the weekly routine. Every week, when my training schedule comes into my inbox, I look to the Sunday run, see the distance and say, *"How am I going to do _____ miles?"* I thought that at 5 miles and every single Sunday that the schedule said more than I had done. My husband just shakes his head and says, "It's just one more than last week!"

While it really is just a little more, Sunday pushes me beyond what I think I'm capable of. It takes me out of my comfort zone and it puts me in community with people who are running beside me but not the same journey.

This is what Sunday has always meant to me — when I set foot in church, when I see God in the challenges and in the wins, when I pray for and beside both strangers and friends, when I meet God at a place I wasn't looking for Him. What I learned Sunday after Sunday, week of doubt after week of doubt, is that **GOD SHOWS UP!** On a quiet neighborhood street with many miles left, He whispered confidence in the journey of all that was behind and all that was to come.

> *Well done, my good and faithful servant. Since you were faithful in small matters, I will give you great responsibilities. Come, share your master's joy.*
>
> *Matthew 25:23 (NABRE)*

God wants to walk through this journey with you. He wants to take your hand and guide you, step-by-step. However, He won't force His presence on you...He wants you to invite Him to walk this journey with you. I encourage you to take a deep breath and place your hand in His. You can count on Him to see you through the entire way! Not only will His companionship encourage you to keep moving forward, He also knows what lies ahead and can give you the strength and endurance to persevere.

Are you deep into a difficult journey?

Do you feel like although you've come a long way, you're still overwhelmed by what lies ahead?

> *"Start by doing what's necessary, then what's possible, and suddenly you are doing the impossible."*
>
> *- Francis of Assisi*

come from a very large extended family — lots of aunts, uncles, cousins, second cousins, and beyond. Most of them live in Maryland, but despite the miles, I've always felt close to them.

This past winter, my cousins, Steve and Irene, lost their oldest daughter, Stefanie, unexpectedly. One week she was mothering her three beautiful children, and the next week, she was gone. Shock and sadness hung on for months, and I watched from afar as they struggled to make sense of this loss. They wrestled with how they would begin to find strength and meaning in this new landscape of life…how they would begin to live their "new normal." I continue to be amazed at how their faith has remained steady, despite their lack of understanding.

I ran my first 16 miles on a Sunday in January without having chosen who I was running for, despite having prayed about it. The entire time I ran, they came into my mind as I felt the love they had for Stefanie and understood that I was a witness to that love as they walked this unknown path and tried to piece together their broken hearts over losing her.

Love is why I am running this marathon: love for Cheryl and wanting to do something **with** her and **for** her, love and obedience to Christ and learning something I didn't know about myself that is beyond

me and for Him, and love for each person He has placed with me on this journey.

And so I dedicate this mile to Steve and Irene and Stefanie because truly, ***our greatest gift is LOVE.***

Pictured above left to right: Steve, Lauren, Stefanie, and Irene

And now these three remain: faith, hope and love. But the greatest of these is love.

I Corinthians 13:13 (NIV)

My MILE

Everyone has an irrational fear. For my daughter, it's needles; for my mom, water; and for me, fire. It's ironic that I live in an area that sees more lightening strikes than the average and the first two years we lived in our house, reports of house fires filled the news — including one in my own neighborhood.

I tend to run a circle so at the beginning, I just ran a loop once and always in the same direction. I'd pass houses and glance at the landscaping and curb appeal, and they became familiar to me. One day, I decided to run the loop in reverse. As I approached a street I knew, but from the opposite direction, I saw a home with a gaping hole. I remembered a report of a fire in our neighborhood about which I had received email requests for both prayers and assistance for the family.

As I studied the house from this new direction, I could see that the entire left side of it was gone. From one angle it looked fine, but from the other, the damage was evident. It had been sitting like that for weeks as the rain came and the sun shone. I assumed it was waiting to be torn down.

I noticed a dumpster one day, and it slowly began to fill. Crews came in and tore out the burned, the water soaked, and the un-repairable parts until all that stood was a shell of the former structure.

Then just as it had been torn apart, it began to be rebuilt. Week after week, I saw the progress and prayed for the people who owned the home. As my miles were advancing, so was the building of this house. I was on my last long run when I saw that it was nearly complete, and it looked very much like a house ready to be occupied.

Sometimes disaster strikes. Sometimes life changes suddenly and drastically, and you have to rebuild it, step-by-step. Sometimes things look whole, but with a different view, we see the damage. Sometimes the only way to make something better is to bring it near it's end and strip it to the bare bones before the rebuilding can happen. Often times, the transformation is a slow, day-by-day change.

This transforming is rarely without discomfort or pain, but what we find is that we have a new structure. What we had might have been good, possibly even great. But what God rebuilds after hardship is even better!

In two weeks I will be running this marathon, not just practicing, but actually IN the race. The thought I had on this run — this image of a complete house — kept my feet moving. Never loose faith in what God can do; keep smiling and give all the glory to Him and Him alone.

Has tragedy struck suddenly in your life?

Have you experienced the destruction of a personal fire — a broken relationship or the death of a loved one or the loss of a career?

Is there a "hole" in your life that can only be seen from a certain angle? Perhaps an area of your life that has remained vacant after you went through a painful trial?

What steps can you take to "strip" this area of your life down to the foundation so that God can rebuild it for HIS purposes and glory?

"I said to the man who stood at the gate of the year, 'Give me a light that I may tread safely into the unknown.' And he replied, 'Go into the darkness and put your hand into the hand of God. That shall be to you better than light and safer than a known way.'"

- Minnie Louise Haskins

73

MILE 17

The Parkers' MILE

met Kevin, the love of my life, when I was 17 years old. When we married, I gained a "second family" — people that I love and who love me in return. I've always said that when it came to parents, I had hit the lottery. But I was the lucky winner who struck gold **twice** — the family I married into is just as special to me as my own family. My sister-in-law, Jenny, picked this verse.

Seventeen miles...this is a number that speaks of commitment. I am ALL IN at this point! To me, committed means that walking away is not an option.

It means staying to finish, even when obstacles occur. This is in marriage or in running or in any marathon in life — all in, every day, in life and in purpose.

This family I chose has been part of the commitment I made at a young age. I'm sure you've heard the quote, "Family is where our story begins." If you can marry into a good family, I would add that it's also where your story becomes a more intricate work of art. Being a part of this "second family" has taken threads of a beautiful story and woven them into even greater beauty.

For this child I prayed and the Lord has granted me my petition which I asked of Him.

1 Samuel 1:27 (NKJV)

I've written about beginnings and I'll write about the end, but usually it's the middle where things get messy and unclear. It's the middle where doubt creeps in and we begin to waver. It's the middle where the hard stuff gets done.

But something else happens in the middle — it's where the people who really mean something show up. They don't just show up for the party at the end... they show up for the work, the tears, the ugly cry, the part of ourselves that is not our best self. That is the middle place.

When I ran miles 14 through 17 in training, I was on my own. They were long, lonely runs. Because it was winter, they were cold and sometimes rainy. Looking around, all I saw were bare trees and dark skies — not a lot of fun to be found. These were hard days of doing hard things.

If given the chance, so often I think I might just skip the middle. However, I don't because I also know it's where the things that are best for us are found. It's where we learn that we are strong... where we learn empathy... where we understand what we can endure and what we are made of where we lean more heavily on God and experience His presence more fully.

That was training. That's what I learned in the preparation.

I have a picture of me on race day in the middle. At mile 15, Cheryl and her family greeted me with signs and smiles and then rode alongside me on their bikes. At mile 17, Cheryl hopped off her bike and ran with me. Like me, she was in the middle of her "something big" — her battle against cancer. She was finished with her surgery and chemotherapy, but she was still facing radiation and reconstruction.

Her journey inspired mine — mine was a chosen challenge, but hers was not. In the middle, we have found people who care, and even when it seems like we're alone, we aren't. God gives us the strength to press on, even through the difficult "middle," and He promises never to leave us.

The middle of cancer...the middle of a marathon... the middle of parent challenges and job losses and infertility and broken marriages...it's in the middle that the hard work happens that propels you forward, dependent on God.

Your MILE

"Middles" are difficult places — far enough in that we don't want to give up, but not far enough that we can feel like we're making real progress. It can be a discouraging place to be...one that can leave us feeling a little lost if we're not careful.

Are you in the "middle" phase of something difficult?

What lessons are you learning in the middle and how can you apply them?

What are 3 small steps you can take this week to help you progress through this challenging phase?

"*Remember, we all stumble, every one of us. That's why it's a comfort to go hand in hand.*"

- Emily Kimbrough

MILE 18

Jen's MILE

For me, Jen has always been filled with God. She lived and spoke of her faith in college when it was "not-so-cool" to do so. She continued to show me her faith as she got married, had kids and went about every day life. This was huge as I began learning to depend on God. She taught me how to weave together the aspects of what we do and what we believe. It was always her dependence on God that amazed me.

Once, when we met for a girls' weekend, she arrived separately from the group and had to make her way to the hotel alone. I remember her saying that she was unsure about the airport and was asking God to help her. I was surprised that she would ask of God such a simple request, but it taught me about daily dependence on God for all things, both big and little.

We have been friends since college — basically, we've grown up together! Not the young years of childhood play — no, the tough years of really figuring out who you are and what your purpose is. Cheryl, Jen and I have been friends for almost 30 years. We are all very different, but in the areas that really matter we are the same — faith, love and friendship!

Early on in this process, I asked Jen what her favorite number was, and she said 18. That is how she came to be the 18th mile. I knew that at this point of the race, I would be in need of long-sustaining prayer. What I didn't know as I was training was that on race day, this verse would be just what I needed to hear as I actually ran 18 miles!

And He has said to me, "My grace is sufficient for you, for power is perfected in weakness." Most gladly, therefore, I will rather boast about my weaknesses, so that the power of Christ may dwell in me. Therefore I am well content with weaknesses, with insults, with distresses, with persecutions, with difficulties, for Christ's sake; for when I am weak, then I am strong.

2 Corinthians 12:9-10 (NASB)

I am a procrastinator. I realize this is not my finest quality, so I try to make this trait of mine have less of an affect on others. Usually that means I work on projects late into the night or take on the bulk of the work on some things. Every once in a while, it backfires. I read a sign at the pharmacy once that said, *"don't make your procrastination my emergency!"* That's where Leah came in...

Early on in this running journey, I had the great idea to have t-shirts made for my family and friends who would be at the race. I knew Leah (who was in my Bible study) did t-shirt graphics, but each week I would miss her and never got the chance to ask her about helping me. I could have easily picked up the phone on any day other than Bible study day...but I didn't.

Just two weeks before race day, I began to realize that my procrastination might not allow for my vision to be realized. Tuesdays are Bible study days and I sat in my quiet time and gave this small detail of matching shirts up as a victim of my bad trait. Wouldn't you know it...guess who I sat next to at Bible study that day?! I discussed my vision with Leah and apologized for not asking her sooner. I explained what the marathon meant to me and why I wanted to run with all 26 verses on my back. I wanted to "carry" each person with me for the entire distance. I wanted anyone who looked to see that this was so much more than just a run. I wanted Cheryl's name to travel the distance that I ran because — in spirit — she had been with me every time I set foot on the road. Leah asked me when I was leaving and when I would need the shirts to be done. After a little calculation, she said we had just enough time if we started that day!

The back and forth of design and layout began, then t-shirt choice, sizes, color and proofing. Leah even drove to the shirt supplier personally to make sure she had time to get them done. As I picked them up right before I flew out, I thanked her again and again. I was so excited to hand them out. It seems kind of silly, I suppose, to be happy about something as insignificant as a t-shirt. However, to me it was once again an answered prayer — it was another reminder that God is in the details!

He looks beyond our character flaws; He's bigger than expectations; He sees the heart of the "why" and answers with His "how." He gives us the people to ask when we need help, but we have to do the asking.

At the 18 mile-mark on race day, I ran on a stretch of road that was filled with people; it was the business district of the area and spectators stretched over the entire mile. I barely saw the strangers because on that mile, I saw my group...my friends and family who were there to cheer me on. They were all decked out in black and pink shirts that matched my own. I stopped for a minute to hug them, and Joshua handed me a flower. They gave words of encouragement and said they were proud of me. It was the whisper I needed from God to say...*it's the journey*. It was loud and clear in pink lettering: who I was running for, why I was running, and all the people who traveled with me on a journey of 26 miles that was so much more than a run!

Your MILE

Don't allow frustrations with your own weaknesses to block you from progressing through the journey He has planned for you! God is so much bigger than you can imagine, and He will help you overcome.

Can you think of a time when God helped you accomplish something despite your own flaws?

If you are in the middle of your own challenging "journey," what markers have you made to identify your progress and help you keep moving forward?

"If you want something you never had, you have to do something you've never done."

- Unknown

Friendship....people come into our lives and change us. They change where we were going and who we become. This mile is dedicated to my friend Gara and her friend Tana. Tana passed away from cancer when she was just 19 years old. Although her life was short, she changed Gara. It was the person she was and the way in which she fought against cancer and eventually succumbed to it that made Gara who she is today.

Gara was one of the moms in my MOMS group. We connected on a spiritual level, and she asked if Tana could be my #19 — even though I had never met her. Seeing how Gara was shaped and impacted by Tana reminds me that friendship is also part of God's plan and that friends in Christ are treasured gifts!

Sometimes when I run, a thought briefly invades my mind that maybe Cheryl won't beat this.

As my running parallels Cheryl's cancer, I also believe that at this point of the run, my body will hurt and it will be hard. If something goes terribly wrong, I might not finish. That is the reality of doing things that challenge us. I know that in running or in cancer or in any uncontrollable situation that we face in life, sometimes God's answer to our prayer is different than what we want. It's in those times that we have to trust that God's plan is good and perfect and that God sees the big picture and we just see the individual details.

I will continue to keep the faith and remember that sometimes the answer is found not in the end, but in the process of getting to the end. It's in the journey that we grow, especially in the valleys.

I have fought the good fight, I have finished the race, I have kept the faith. Now there is in store for me the crown of righteousness, which the Lord the righteous Judge, will award to me on that day — and not only to me, but also to all who have longed for his appearing.

2 Timothy 4:7-8 (NIV)

My MILE

For my entire life, I've heard stories about Skip, my Dad's college roommate from the Naval Academy. However, I had never met him in person. When I told my parents that the race was in Jacksonville, FL, they decided to come cheer me on since that is where Skip and his wife, Beverly, live. They have a grown son (Chris) who is an ultra marathoner and he lives there as well. He had helped other people run in races by coming along side them for the hard miles, and he said he would do the same for me even though we had never met. I appreciated the help and decided, "the more, the merrier!"

At 19 miles, I got kind of quiet. My foot hurt and I was getting cranky. I was trying to put on a good act, but inside, I was doubting how this body of mine was going to cover 7 ½ more miles. Chris had just joined us and he was full of spirit. He told us stories of his 100+ mile runs and gave helpful encouragement. He knew the course and direction and began giving me goals to shoot for, combinations of walking and running that kept me moving forward.

In so many situations in life, we need someone who has done what we are doing to come alongside us, keep us motivated, give advice, and provide whatever it is we need. But in order for this to happen, we have to be open to the help. We have to admit weakness and the need for another person to bear the burden — not **FOR** us but **WITH** us.

This is hard to do in our culture of "the pretty and perfect" lives on social media where we only show the good and the fun and rarely the hard and messy side of things. At this point in the race, I was beginning to fade and falter, but I found that what I needed most was not to rely on myself. What I needed most was to yield. At mile 19, I yielded to Chris' knowledge of running. I allowed him to take over the control of pace and progress.

I've found that it's that way in life, too. It is only when I let go of my control and yield to God's way that the path seems manageable and I'm able to experience peace right where I am despite the distance I still have to cover. It doesn't make the distance shorter, and it doesn't make the pain go away. It makes it manageable. It's about slowing down and sharing the burdens while still doing hard things.

Years ago, when I understood who God was in my life, I made the decision to yield to Him. What I learn with every turn of the road and every new challenge in life is that this is a daily act of being in the mind set of. . . *let go and let God!*

Your MILE

There's no shame in allowing others to come alongside and help you — in fact, it's how God designed it. He wants us to share the ups and downs of life together!

Are you trying to "run your race" on your own?

Do you accept help offered by others?

Do you struggle with setting aside your pride and admitting you need help?

"The secret of change is to focus all of your energy, not on fighting the old, but on building the new."

- Socrates

MILE 20

Gena's MILE

This is Gena's mile. We were friends in the 10th grade, and after I moved away that sophomore year, we didn't keep in touch. I hadn't seen or talked to her since I was 16. Fast-forward 20+ years and she "friended" me on social media. You know how when you first sign up, you look up every person you ever knew?! Well, that was how our friendship was renewed.

I began to see posts about tests and scans and asking for prayer. She had cancer and shared her journey on social media because she knows so many people from around the world. I watched from afar as she continued to trust and praise God in all things — both the miracles and the setbacks.

After a second round of cancer, she was in remission and praised God by walking the NYC marathon and raising over $10,000 for cancer research. A video of her crossing the finish line brought tears to my eyes.

I emailed Gena and asked her to be my 20th mile, explaining what I was doing and why. She lives in Scotland, but even from that distant place, she took time to provide for me this verse and her support.

Her faithfulness inspired me beyond words. Every post she wrote and every step of the journey that God has taken her on ended with these words, "The best is yet to come." So I will be inspired by this and remember to praise God, even when there is pain.

To read more about Gena's powerful story, visit the website www.MoreThanAMile.org

In marathon training, or at least in my case, the longest training run I was to do was 20 miles. It marked the end of training before the recovery transition to race day. The idea is that you let your body rest a bit so that it's a well-conditioned and well-restored machine on race day.

I still worried about the last 6.2 miles, but Coach Loran said at that point, I could walk the rest if I had to!

On long run days, my stomach was always a mess of nerves. I hemmed and hawed before finally getting outside to begin. I knew this run would be long, and my friend Laura met me for about 5 miles in the middle to encourage me. But by the end of that run, I was by myself again. I was on a stretch of road that I run on repeatedly. Every house...every tree was familiar. My finish line that day was my street, GRACELAND.

On that final training day, as I approached the last stretch, there were no cheering crowds or familiar faces smiling at what I had accomplished. I was exhausted and all alone — trust me, it wasn't pretty! But then I turned onto Graceland and realized, "I'm home." All the running and striving and pushing myself had led to this moment. My finish line that day was GRACE — God's grace.

Even when this marathon is over and I run under the "FINISH" banner, I will remember that the bigger, grander plan of life — the race I am TRULY running — is a race for eternity. Beyond this day, this season, this trial, is our true journey.

When I reach the "finish line" of my life, I will see Jesus face-to-face, and only by God's grace will I be home in heaven...my eternal "GRACE LAND."

Because your steadfast love is better than life, my lips will praise you.

Psalm 63:3 (ESV)

Your MILE

At some point, each of us will be in the "home stretch" of our life. God offers grace and mercy to those who believe that Jesus paid for their sins when He died on the cross. **That is truly amazing grace.**

Have you put your faith in Jesus? If not, I encourage you to do it today. None of us knows how many days we'll be given here on earth, so don't delay. This is too important of a decision!

It's simple to do...simply talk to God and tell Him that you know you have messed up and that you want to accept Jesus' gift of forgiveness and salvation. There aren't any "special" words to say... God knows your heart!

If you just accepted Jesus as your personal Savior, would you please send me a note? I would love to connect with you and send you a few resources to help you get started in your new spiritual journey with God!

Here's how you can contact us:

info@lifemarkministries.org
LifeMark Ministries
2001 W. Plano Pkwy, Suite 3403
Plano, TX 75075

We would love to hear from you so please take a moment and contact us!

"We shall not cease from exploring, and the end of our exploring will be to arrive where we started and know the place for the first time."

- *T.S. Eliot*

MILE 21

Claire's MILE

ew territory! I trained up to 20 miles, so every mile after 20 will be a discovery of new challenges on race day.

My baby girl is 21 this year. This is Claire's mile. For 21 years, I've had the privilege of being a mother. I know that at times I have not done it well, but I also know that through it all, I have experienced a love that cannot be described.

In January, as Claire studied abroad in Paris, she was swept into a world event as she dealt with the terror attacks that occurred right where she was. It was an extremely stressful situation, and she found herself being torn between feelings of wanting to retreat to safety versus finish what she had started. It was a significant "grown-up" decision. She wanted me to tell her what to do, but we have transitioned from the role of decision maker to the role of advisor in her life. This was a choice that she had to make on her own. With courage, she decided to stay, despite her extreme fear and unease.

When she returned home, she told me she was glad she stayed. I was so proud of her. As I ran this mile — this new place for me — I realized that some things are just hard. We can choose to skip around them or to move through them. However, it is in those hard places that we rely not on ourselves but on others and on God. He shows up!

She googled a Bible verse on courage and came across Deuteronomy 31:6. This verse marks a significant transition from Moses leading the nation of Israel to Joshua leading them. It is both a place of ending and a place of beginning. And so at 21, my little girl has stepped a foot onto the path of adulthood, and in doing so, she has given me courage to go beyond where I thought possible.

Be strong and of good courage, do not fear nor be afraid of them; for the Lord your God, He is the the One who goes with you. He will not leave you nor forsake you.

Deuteronomy 31:6 (NKJV)

My MILE

As I ran this mile on race day — a new place — I thought about the fact that some things are just hard and I turned a corner, both literally and figuratively. I ran from busy, people-filled streets to the local main road that would eventually take me to the finish line. The road was uneven and strewn with rocks, cracks, and narrow spots. The strangers who ran alongside me in the race became familiar as I passed them and they passed me.

Hard places require perseverance and obedience.

When I first thought about doing this marathon for Cheryl, I knew it would be beyond running. Early on, I was asked why I didn't just do a half-marathon. My answer was that I was pretty sure I could do that. It wouldn't be easy, but it was doable.

For me, 26 miles was the number that seemed beyond me, a place that God would need to bring me to. I knew 26 miles would leave me completely dependent on God to get me through the hard places. It wasn't something I wanted to do — in fact, I strongly did NOT want to do it! But God called me out of my area of comfort and told me to trust Him. It would be hard, but it would be beautiful.

What I found was not the answers lined up, neat and orderly. No, it was an unfolding of the plan. I could not have imagined the end when I began. I did not know that I would carry with me 26 verses given by 26 people that corresponded to the 26 miles. I did not know that the feeling of accomplishing something by completely depending on God could revive and not drain. I did not know at the beginning that Cheryl would run part of this race with me.

But what I DID know was that God, when invited in, is greater than all the doubts, fears, and obstacles. He brings us to new places to show us His glory.

Your MILE

Just a few miles ago, we talked about the how the "middles" of our marathons are difficult places and that we have to be careful we don't stall out. At this point, we're past the "difficult" and fully enveloped by the "hard." At this point of the journey, we must face our doubts, fears, and obstacles by continuing to put one foot in front of the other and trusting in God to get us through.

When has fear waged war in your life?

What struggle requires you to "be strong and of good courage" in order to face it and move forward?

"When you come to the end of all the light you know and it's time to step into the darkness of the unknown, faith is knowing that one of two things will happen: either you will be given something solid to stand on or you will be taught to fly."

- Patrick Overton

MILE 22

Laura's MILE

Being new to Texas, I don't have a support system of friends to call. In Iowa I ran with friends — it was one of the few things that made running tolerable! I'm a slow runner so a running group intimidates me, which meant I was going to have to train on my own. Thankfully, God brought me Laura.

Laura is my "God is in the details" friend. I wrote about meeting her in the 6th mile lesson. The circumstance of our meeting seemed at the time so random. What I came to understand was that she was a gift.

Knowing I was going to meet her on Sundays helped motivate me to move past the fear of the actual number of miles on my training plan. Since she was not training for anything (just helping me), as the miles got higher she would end the runs with me. It was something to look forward to.

The first time we met was at a social, so we were dressed in business casual with our makeup and hair fixed. Every other time after that was in workout gear with no make-up and pony-tails!

In our daily lives, we are mostly opposites. She has a great career filled with work attire, meetings, business travel and a paycheck. As a stay-at-home mom, my days are filled with tees and jeans, playgrounds and carpools.

Externally we seem a bit opposite, but that is not the case. At the heart of where friendship is truly born, it is the common ground you share. As we ran, we talked about kids and life, relationships and dreams...things you typically talk about with friends. But beyond all of this, we talked about faith, sharing where God has been and how He has moved in our lives.

Running week after week allowed me to share my faith and journey with her and reminded me that in this life, we are called to walk with one another. Early on, I asked Laura for her favorite number and she said 22. It seems appropriate that she would be in a place I had never been before...yep, God is in the details!

My MILE

Early in the training process, I developed a nagging irritation on my foot. Most days it was fine, but after long run days, I would limp around for most of the morning. As the runs got longer, the annoyance of my foot would last the entire day. I knew I should see a doctor to have it checked, but I also knew the doctor would tell me to rest…and that was not an option! So after I ran, I would apply ice and essential oils and just deal with it.

My husband, who does triathlons, said it was my visit to the "pain cave." This was his way of saying, when you push yourself you have to suffer. I'm not good with this concept. I told him I birthed 3 kids — I had put in my time suffering by choice.

But here I was — suffering by choice, again.

Suffering is a hard concept when we choose to do it ourselves. It's even more difficult when we watch someone we love suffer. It is a place that makes us begin to question all that we believe and all that we feel is important. It is also where we have to really focus and dig deep into all that we have, remembering the important lessons we've stored up for just this kind of moment.

Somewhere in those long miles, when my body screamed to stop but my heart would not allow it, I realized suffering and love often melt together when we give up our comfort for the needs of someone else. This is on a person-to-person basis, but even broader, when we submit to God's will in our lives.

In a place of suffering, we begin to focus on small details, small needs and small answers. Pulling the focus even wider, I am humbled and grateful for a Savior who would go to the cross to suffer for me.

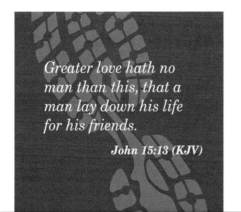

Greater love hath no man than this, that a man lay down his life for his friends.

John 15:13 (KJV)

Your MILE

Suffering yourself or watching someone you love suffer is heartbreaking. It often drives us to withdraw into an isolated setting where others won't see our struggle. But suffering is a natural part of living in this world. It can be difficult to reconcile the suffering we experience or witness with a sovereign God who loves us and wants the best for us. How can that be? We need only look to the cross for that answer. God was willing to send His only Son to SUFFER and DIE an excruciating death in order to pay the price for our sins. Through His own suffering, God gives us the opportunity to spend eternity with Him where there will be no more suffering and no more pain.

In light of that gift, we have the power (through HIM) to persevere through our pain. What pain are you experiencing that you need to push through?

Have you accepted God's help to get you through this season of suffering?

"*I am only one, but still I am one. I cannot do everything, but still I can do something; and because I cannot do everything, I will not refuse to do something that I can do.*"

- Edward Everett Hale

ebi and I aren't old friends, but we were fast friends. In all the new challenges and changes we faced moving to Texas, it has been Debi who has brought many good things into my life and has been an incredible blessing.

We started our friendship first through business when our family began the process of house hunting in Texas because Debi was our realtor. You cover a variety of topics with your realtor, especially when moving to a new state. Once our realtor / client relationship was over, we developed a deeper friendship.

In an unfamiliar community where no one even knew my name, she was the person who knew my story. She had walked in my shoes years before when she was new to Texas and made sure that each week, I was adjusting and finding my way.

She insisted that I go to her Bible study, and that group has blessed and enriched my life. On days that were especially hard, Debi has been there with encouraging words or hands to help. I knew she would be one of my miles and as the runs got longer I knew I wanted her to be a tough mile. I figured that because she's been there for me so many times this year, somewhere near the end of this crazy marathon journey seemed appropriate.

She's gone the distance with me, and this tough place would be no different.

My MILE

I have a theory about service to others: JUST SHOW UP! I guard my time fiercely, so this is a bit of a challenge for me. I'm selfish and stingy about giving my free time away, and that leads to being one of those people who never volunteers for things.

Early one morning, as I was running, I looked up on a power-line to see two birds sitting side-by-side. The morning sun was just peeking out, and I was praying for Cheryl. I thought about the two of us sitting next to each other as friends all these years, but today the miles made it impossible for me to sit next to her...to crack jokes and make her smile as she went through her chemo treatments.

But this running, this training, this praying was my way of "showing up." The marathon has been our line, our life line of friendship. When my alarm clock rings, I lace up my sneakers and run. As I do, I pray and text her to let her know...this has been our connection... how I "showed up" for her through cancer.

The idea of "showing up" is an act of "doing" — doing something not at YOUR convenience, but in THEIR need. It's about using your time, energy, skill, or ability to help in some small way. It's not about how big the act is; it's about the obedience of using what you've been given to benefit someone else.

"Showing up" sometimes begins with grumbling at the idea of an interruption in your day or your year or even your life. But I've discovered that "showing up" is not the nuisance...*it's actually the purpose*. Half of my year was dedicated to expending time, energy, and money for Cheryl. However, during that process, God gave me lessons that filled in the blanks of so many questions I had been asking.

Sometimes you are the one who shows up; other times you receive the gift of another showing up for you. In this give and take, God shows Himself and reveals what only He can do. He takes the little we have and turns it into abundance beyond belief!

> *Whatever you do, work at it with all your heart, as working for the Lord, not for human masters.*
>
> **Colossians 3:23 (NIV)**

Your MILE

In a society that doesn't regard commitment very highly, "showing up" for someone takes intentionality, courage, and love. It's something we should strive to do in order to bless others in their marathons...and often, we'll be blessed ourselves in the process!

Who has "shown up" in your life? How can you thank them today?

Who have you "shown up" for and what did that look like?

Is God calling you to "show up" for someone right now? What do you need to let go of to follow Him?

"Ask not for an easy life...ask for the strength to face the elements, to weather the storms; to be the might for the right and the weak; to be the voice for those who cannot speak, to see one's dreams to fruition with dignity, integrity and grace."

- *Giac Nguyen*

MILE 24

Kim's MILE

My sister Kim chose the verse for this mile. Years ago, someone very special to her was killed in Iraq. Just a kid, he had come into her life for the very important purpose of restoring a fractured relationship. For that reason, she keeps his memory alive.

For many years now, Kim has suffered with multiple diseases. If you met her, you would think she was attractive, always put together, and friendly. What you wouldn't see is that she is almost always in pain. She puts on a brave face but usually feels awful.

I hate this for her. I hate that chronic pain is just part of her daily life, and for now, she just manages it. But she's found outlets for distraction — she's creative, crafty and talented. It is in these things that I see her soul — the person she is without the constant pain.

Twenty-four miles is hard and so I will use this mile to just trudge through to find a positive distraction and let that push me forward. I will look for the bright light to focus on...just like Kim does!

> Greater love hath no man than this, that a man lay down his life for his friend.
>
> *John 15:13 (KJV)*

My MILE

Dig deep…see only the goal…lean in to all that you know to be true…it's painful and pain hurts — these were the lessons at Mile 24. I knew at this point that I was going to finish. If I had to crawl on my hands and knees the last 2 miles, I would cross the finish line. However, the place where I was required pain, and it was just a matter of figuring out how the pain would shape the next 2 miles.

We were on uneven pavement, my nagging foot injury had moved into intense pain, and I could see the only up hill in the race was ahead of me. This was the hardest mile.

As my current challenges faced me, I was not alone. Both Chris and Cheryl were beside me giving me moral support. I asked Cheryl at that point to tell me about her hardest cancer day because I wanted to refocus and mentally move from my discomfort to her strength.

She shared with me about a day that was supposed to be a "normal" chemo treatment that had gone horribly wrong. She had an unexpected allergic reaction to a new medication and her throat began to swell suddenly. She understandably panicked because she couldn't breathe. Thankfully, she and the nurse had discussed this unusual reaction right before they started the new drug. It had seemed like a meaningless conversation at the time, but it prompted the nurse to have an EPI pen on-hand just in case so she was able to intervene quickly and Cheryl was able to breathe again. Praise God!

After hearing her story, I felt like my foot and my uphill climb were not quite as bad as I had thought! I've heard it said before that when you're struggling, doing something for someone else helps ease the pain because it allows you to see your circumstances differently and refocus on what really matters. I used this idea not only on the 24th mile, but really throughout the entire 26-mile journey.

Because each mile told a story, each mile required that my mind shift from one person to the next and reflect on how they fit in the entire plan. It was the reason I was doing the marathon — so that my pain (training and running) could connect with Cheryl's pain (cancer and radiation and fighting for her life.) Ultimately, God used this lesson to help both of us focus on how He could shape and use our pain to show us His goodness in all things, even on the hardest mile.

Pain will come — it's just part of our human experience. When it comes, take a moment to refocus. See who is with you, helping you carry the load. Ask someone about their struggle and learn how they survived. Reach out to another whose pain may be worse than yours.

Are you in a painful situation right now? Are you overwhelmed with difficult circumstances?

Who needs your help to push through their own pain? Who can you encourage?

"*The ultimate measure of a man is not where he stands in moments of comfort and convenience, but where he stands at times of challenge and controversy.*"

- Martin Luther King, Jr.

MILE 25

Kevin's MILE

A t 17 I met him, and at 23 I married him. For 25 years, Kevin has been my husband. He is my best friend, my greatest cheerleader, the hand that lifts me up, and the shoulder I cry on. He is the partner I will share my life with.

I would like to say that for 25 years, we've been blissfully happy. But in real relationship, that is just not true. We have seen ups and downs, laughter and tears, joys and sorrow. Sometimes, and for that matter some years, things have not been pretty, but in the end, we are left with beautiful imperfection that continues to strive for better, not perfect.

Twenty-five miles is a LONG way to run, but God has shown me that sometimes it is when we go the distance and allow Him to be the main focus, anything is possible.

When I started researching possible marathons to run, I had three criteria: 1) a breast cancer marathon, 2) located on the east coast (so Cheryl could be there), and 3) at least 6 months to train. The Donna Run came up in my online search, and it was in Florida in February — perfect! The absolute bonus was it was considered one of the flattest courses and really beautiful, even including a stretch of beach running. That was the answer to the question, *"Where?"*.

Remember earlier when I wrote that I hate to run? Well I've learned to endure running, but I really, really hate hills!

So when I got to Mile 25 I literally began to laugh — the only hill of the entire race was at Mile 25! It was an enormous bridge that took you over the water to get you to the other side to the finish line. I texted Kevin at that point to tell him it was the only uphill. . . his mile. He loves hills.

His reply was, *"that's where you pass people."* Well, I didn't pass anyone, but it did make me think.

I've stood on many mountaintops — high above tree lines — and taken in the view. I am always awed by God's design and diversity and beauty. It is from above things that we see them in their entirety. When the pieces of the view all come into form, we see how they work together to create unique beauty. This is the top. But to get there we have to go uphill. It's hard work, and it requires that we endure.

If I think back to places in my life where I've found the most beauty, I can look and see that before that moment, I had been working hard to get there. The process of going through the valley and facing the uphill climb brings you to God's presence, the answers to the questions that seemed unanswerable, and ultimately to God's will for your life.

Whatever your mountain, remember there is work and struggle and hard days, but at the top. . .*ohhhhh, the view you will find!*

> *Do you not know that in a race all the runners run, but only one gets the prize? Run in such a way as to get the prize. Everyone who competes in the games goes into strict training. They do it to get a crown that will not last, but we do it to get a crown that will last forever.*
>
> *1 Corinthians 9:24-25 (NIV)*

Your MILE

Wouldn't it be nice if we could avoid uphill climbs in life? Maybe we could just take a gondola or chair lift up the hill to enjoy the views from the top? But life isn't usually like that, is it. Generally speaking, we have to climb uphill in order to enjoy the mountaintop experience . . . *and there's purpose in that process.*

What mountain or hill lies ahead of you?

Who can you reach out to that will help you keep moving upward?

Who needs your assistance to climb the hill they are facing?

"The highest reward for man's toil is not what he gets for it but what he becomes by it."

— *John Ruskin*

I've been going to Bible study at Kristie's house since my first week in Texas. We have a workbook lesson that we complete at home, and then we meet for a small group discussion followed by a lecture.

In the past, we watched taped versions of the lecture, but this year, Mark (the Bible Study teacher) gives the talk to our group in person. Every week, something he says stays with me. Lots of things make sense or teach me, but always one real-life, relevant detail ruminates in my mind all week.

For all the months I've been training, I thought my final verse would be this — "all things are possible with God" and that is true, so very true. But as I listened to the lecture just 2 weeks before the marathon, a different verse struck me... Mark 11:23.

I had always envisioned this verse in light of God's power. I could see a mountain literally moving — one minute, it's over here and another minute, it's over there. I was content with the sense of not understanding the "how" but knowing the "Who." But in the lecture, Mark said sometimes God moves mountains one wheel barrel at a time and the moving of that mountain takes years.

I realized that was the journey of this marathon. In July, I could barely run one mile. I had no idea when I began what would unfold between July and February, how Cheryl would fight cancer and be healed, how I

would get from mile 1 to the finish line at mile 26, or how the journey would include so many other people. I just knew that God had directed me to move a mountain.

My life is about faith...about hearing God's voice in all the things that I do. He always asks me to do things for Him that I think are beyond what I can do on my own. What I keep finding is that when I see Him in those moments, when I listen and obey, He always provides the people and the strength to accomplish His task.

In training, I did loops. I passed places that I had been over and over. As I added miles, I'd make the loop bigger so even a new place became familiar week after week as the miles increased. It was safe and practical because I knew what to expect. I knew where I could rest, grab a drink, and catch my breath.

Race day was different. It was new and unchartered in many ways. I had to trust the signs and the people around me. I did not know what was ahead, but I went forward with confidence that the way was clear and safe.

I mostly like safe. I like knowing the path I'm going to take and what landmarks I will see along the way, but here's what race day taught me: **The unknown path is amazing.**

I ran on busy highways and quiet neighborhood streets. I ran alone. I ran surrounded by strangers. I smiled at people who yelled my name. I stood in awe as the sun sparkled on the everchanging waves hitting the surf and on the shifting sand of the beach. Strangers gave encouragement, and those I loved were waiting at the finish line.

I had not placed my feet onto that ground before, and most likely, I never will again. But I would never trade that unknown journey of 26 miles for all of the "familiar" journeys in all the days to follow.

Finding beauty in ordinary is sometimes the hardest thing to do. Yet as I look back over all the steps I took in this seemingly impossible dream, I can see that the journey makes us open ourselves to trusting in God's plan — whether familiar or completely new. He fills in the blanks, checks all the boxes, and completes the unknowns of the story. He brings beauty from it all.

> *Truly I tell you, if anyone says to this mountain, 'Go throw yourself into the sea' and does not doubt in their heart but believes that what they say will happen, it will be done for them. Therefore I tell you, whatever you ask for in prayer, believe that you have received it, and it will be yours.*
>
> *Mark 11:23-24 (NIV)*

Your MILE

Going "off-road" can be scary, but the adventures found on the unknown path stretch us and mold us into the people God wants us to be. Our safety lies not in knowing our circumstances but in knowing our Creator.

Does the thought of unknown territory scare you?

Is God calling you to do something beyond what you can do, requiring you to be fully dependent on Him?

What mountain are you facing that is so big you need to just focus on moving one wheelbarrow of dirt at a time?

"You have been assigned this mountain top to show others it can be moved."

- Unknown

Marathon **DAY**

*O*n a beautiful and slightly chilly morning in February, I woke up with anticipation for THE day. Clothes, shoes, food, and water bottles were all laid out ready to be grabbed. I headed to the destination — the start line. I was surrounded by hundreds of strangers with one thing in common: on that day, we shared the same path, although our journey getting there was different.

As we all began, I knew that some standing there would finish and some would not. Truth be told, I did not know which group I would be in! On my back, printed in pink were 26 Bible verses, each given and received in love, in gratitude and in prayer. To say I was nervous barely touches on the scope of my emotion. It was my goal that day to take it all in, to pay attention, to listen, to smile, to enjoy and just complete what I had practiced.

You may recall on Day 2 of this journey, I shared with you how God forced me to face my weak spots — lack of structure and discipline, love of sweets, and finishing long projects. At this point, I knew I had **prepared well**. I had trained with structure and discipline, and I had made healthy choices to put me in a good position to **finish well**.

But, as with all things, I also expected the unexpected. There would be places where I would have to adjust and pivot and, well, just make it up as I went along.

At the end of the first mile, I knew that my body was a little off, but I chalked it up to nerves. Unfortunately it was not nerves, but issues…tummy issues to be exact. So my well-constructed plan got altered quickly. From miles 1 to 8, I ran alone. As I began mile 9, panic over my tummy issues began to take a toll on me emotionally. And that's when God sent Kevin to meet me. He thought he was going to just give me a quick high five, but he obviously could see my distress so he ran with me for the next 7 miles. He helped me adjust and refocus and keep me on track.

As we got to mile 16, Cheryl, her husband and 3 kids were there to greet me on their bikes with signs and cheers. Then at 17 miles, Cheryl hopped off her bike and ran with me, beside me for the rest of the way. In a pause between chemo and radiation she had regained some of her strength, and because I run slow, we could pace together. The beauty of that does not escape me — God allowed us to share part of the path together, literally side-by-side. Then a special group of friends met me with hugs and smiles at mile 18 — exactly when doubt was pushing in because I still had a long way before I was done. God gave me the gift of those who know me and love me to push me forward and give me strength.

The miles between seeing those I loved and the finish line were filled with strangers — some looked strong and others struggled. We encouraged each other, gave knowing smiles, and tried to make the journey just a bit better.

Then it was before me, a place that I had envisioned without the certainty of seeing. Every step taken, every mile practiced and recorded was behind me, and I sprinted under a banner that read FINISH.

FINISH: *bring(a task or activity) to an end: complete*

That sounds so definite and final. The discipline of running, the structure of schedules and water intake, the rotation of shoes, etc — everything in the preparation phase was completed at the finish line. *I had finished well!*

But the impact of the marathon went beyond that single day because through this difficult journey, **I was CHANGED**. Changed by all the lessons I learned along the way. Changed by the knowledge that God would supply all that I needed, despite my own fears

and doubts. Changed by all the people who had traveled the 26.2 miles with me, both in preparation as well as on marathon day.

When we travel a road that is long and hard but unselfish and purposeful, rooted in obedience and uncertainty, we find meaning as we stop to see the places where it was touched by God.

If this is how we viewed every "marathon" set before us, by seeing God's glory displayed over and over, then glancing back at the distance we've come and be certain that we are loved, we are known and we are held by an amazing God, then we have accomplished the goal set before us.

Your MILE

The "marathons" we go through in life change us...sometimes in small ways that only we notice... other times in significant ways that alter our future path. They push us beyond what we can handle and force us to rely on God to get us through. Each marathon strengthens us for the next one in this journey of life.

As you reflect on your 30-day journey, what lessons have you learned that have changed you?

Do you feel different about your "marathon" now than you did at the beginning?

"Some things have to be believed
to be seen."

- Madeleine L'Engle

One Journey ENDS & Another BEGINS

It's always made me laugh that marathons are 26.2 miles...as if 26 miles isn't enough! But here is what I learned about that last fifth of a mile: It's where the crowds formed clapping and yelling; it's where smiles were everywhere — smiles of relief, of pride, and of joy; it's where the party music played — upbeat and exciting; and it's where hugs and tears abounded!

The ".2" is where you know definitely, absolutely that you are going to finish. So how about those marathons that don't involve running?

In "life marathons" that are filled with broken hearts or broken dreams or stress-filled sleepless nights, what do those ".2" moments look and feel like? I would submit that they are similar. There's a sense of accomplishment and pride for having survived the journey along with an overwhelming feeling of relief that the worst is behind you.

I think that ".2" seasons are sweet gifts from God. They are opportunities to catch your breath, recognize you're almost to the finish line, and celebrate with those who love you. Though short-lived, these ".2" seasons are incredibly important to keeping us moving forward! If you are still in your marathon, keep pressing on — your ".2" season lies ahead! You can do it with God's grace and help!

Hebrews 12:1-3 describes these ".2" seasons of life well. As you read these words, picture the last .2 of a mile in the marathon: you're exhausted but re-energized as you run for the finish line... surrounded by crowds cheering and clapping:

"Therefore, since we are surrounded by such a great cloud of witnesses, let us throw off everything that hinders and the sin that so easily entangles. And let us run with perseverance the race marked out for us, fixing our eyes on Jesus, the pioneer and perfecter of faith. For the joy set before him he endured the cross, scorning its shame, and sat down at the right hand of the throne of God. Consider him who endured such opposition from sinners, so that you will not grow weary and lose heart." (NIV)

Take heart and press on!

Thank you for taking this journey with me...a journey of two girls, really — one who hated running but was able to travel 26.2 miles one step at a time, and one who didn't have time for cancer but slowed down and saw God's healing touch beyond her physical illness.

On that February day, we accomplished an amazing feat — we saw God's glory. Later that same year on a crisp fall day, Cheryl's doctor gave her an "all clear" as he shared an official remission diagnosis. We had both made it through our journeys — though they were different, they were intertwined. We've been blessed by more years of health, friendship and memories with one another.

In that season, God taught us about different ways to do a marathon and the lessons learned along the way. But I use the word "season" because we never are just "one and done." Oh the joy if we all just had one good marathon to run! But growth is not found in standing still or in staying put. My greatest journey has been learning how I can be a light for Christ...how I can be molded and surrendered to all the marathons each season brings and how to learn from each one and carry those lessons into future marathons in life.

At the end of the The Donna Marathon, I clapped my hands, thanked God for the blessings and declared, "I will never do that again!" HA!

God was not done with the story of our shared marathon. The Donna Marathon started as a way I could support and encourage Cheryl. What came next was to be traveled WITH Cheryl - but that is a tale for another day and one more journey that took us...

more than a mile.

Your MILE

Congratulations on completing this journey! Although the road is difficult, persevering to the end brings incredible relief and joy.

How can you use the ".2" seasons in your life to help propel you forward to the finish line and beyond into your next marathon?

What lessons did you learn that will carry over into your next marathon?

"Isn't it funny how day by day nothing changes. But when you look back, everything is different?"

- C.S. Lewis

Congratulations!

You have completed this 30-day journey — great job! We pray that you have been challenged by what you have learned and grown closer to God as you've progressed through your own "marathon."

It's important that you don't stop now! Here are some suggestions to help you continue to grow:

Daily Prayer: Start each day with prayer. It's a conversation between you and God. Talk with Him about your day. Praise Him and share your concerns. Ask Him to fill you with His Spirit and guide your decisions each day. Strive to keep Him at the forefront of your thoughts.

Daily Bible Reading: Reading the Bible is essential to growing closer to God and living a fulfilling life. We have some reading programs on our website to help guide you. Or you can start by reading through the Psalms and Proverbs each day. If you want to learn more about Jesus, spend some time reading through the books of Matthew, Mark, Luke, and John. Regardless of where you start — the important thing is to start today!

Start a Bible Study: We have a variety of studies available, including some of Paul's letters as well as an in-depth study on the life of Jesus called ***Mosaic of the Master (volumes I and II)***. There are also a number of excellent Bible studies available at your local Christian bookstore or online. Regardless of which one you select, the important thing is to study His Word!

Visit our Website: There you will find additional studies, tips, encouragement, and resources to help you in your walk with God. Visit our blog for devotionals and announcements, and follow us on Facebook and Twitter for daily encouragement.

Sign-up for Mondays with Mark: Our weekly video devotional will help you begin your week in God's Word. These 2-minute videos arrive in your email inbox every Monday morning. To learn more, visit **www.MondaysWithMark.org**

A believer's **LifeMark** is the *legacy* left by a life spent *loving* and *serving* God and man.
LifeMark Ministries exists to help people discover that the Bible is
alive, active, and applicable.
We help people *learn* God's Word so they can boldly *live* His Word...for His glory!
This is our calling and our passion. This is our LifeMark. What's yours?
To learn more about this ministry, visit our website: **www.LifeMarkMinistries.org**

67871750R00071

Made in the USA
Columbia, SC
02 August 2019